Writing Undergraduate Lab Reports
A Guide for Students

Writing clear, impactful reports is a crucial skill for science students, but few books focus on this area for the undergraduate. Particularly useful for biology students, this text adopts a hands-on approach, using example reports and published papers as models to put guidance into practice. An introductory chapter familiarizes undergraduates with the principles of writing science. Two model reports are then developed, walking students through experimental and observational teaching-lab reports. The structure and content of Introduction, Methods and Materials, Results, and Discussion are explained, together with tips for the title, abstract, and references. Students are then guided to polish their first draft. The last section of the book analyzes two published papers, helping the reader transition to reporting original research. Clearly and concisely written, this text offers a much-needed lifeline for science students facing science report-writing for the first time, and for those looking to hone their writing skills.

Christopher S. Lobban is Professor Emeritus of Biology at the University of Guam, where he taught scientific writing and biology. He delights in writing and has contributed to many research publications and several books, including *Seaweed Ecology and Physiology* (Cambridge University Press 2014), the second edition of which won the Phycological Society of America's Prescott Book Award.

María Schefter earned her PhD in Sociolinguistics of Science. Her work spans language education and biology; she brings her expertise in both to this text. She has co-authored several books and research papers with Professor Lobban.

Writing Undergraduate Lab Reports
A Guide for Students

Christopher S. Lobban
University of Guam

María Schefter
University of Guam

CAMBRIDGE
UNIVERSITY PRESS

CAMBRIDGE
UNIVERSITY PRESS

University Printing House, Cambridge CB2 8BS, United Kingdom

One Liberty Plaza, 20th Floor, New York, NY 10006, USA

477 Williamstown Road, Port Melbourne, VIC 3207, Australia

4843/24, 2nd Floor, Ansari Road, Daryaganj, Delhi – 110002, India

79 Anson Road, #06–04/06, Singapore 079906

Cambridge University Press is part of the University of Cambridge.

It furthers the University's mission by disseminating knowledge in the pursuit of education, learning, and research at the highest international levels of excellence.

www.cambridge.org
Information on this title: www.cambridge.org/9781107117402
DOI: 10.1017/9781316338575

First published 2017

Printed in the United Kingdom by Clays, St Ives plc

A catalogue record for this publication is available from the British Library.

Library of Congress Cataloging-in-Publication Data
Names: Lobban, Christopher S., author. | Schefter, Maria, author.
Title: Writing undergraduate lab reports : a guide for students / Christopher
    S. Lobban, University of Guam, Maria Schefter, University of Guam.
Description: New York, NY : Cambridge University Press, 2017. | Includes
    bibliographical references and index.
Identifiers: LCCN 2017028165 | ISBN 9781107117402 (alk. paper)
Subjects: LCSH: Technical writing – Handbooks, manuals, etc. | Communication
    in science – Handbooks, manuals, etc. | Report writing – Handbooks, manuals,
    etc.
Classification: LCC T11 .L625 2017 | DDC 808.06/65–dc23
LC record available at https://lccn.loc.gov/2017028165

ISBN 978-1-107-11740-2 Hardback
ISBN 978-1-107-54024-8 Paperback

In memory of our parents:
Olwyn Ursula Lobban (1920–2009) and James Lobban (1920–1990)
Dorothy F. Schefter (1909–1987) and Elmer Frances Schefter (1909–1977)

Contents

Acknowledgments

In the 25 years since we wrote *Successful Lab Reports*, on which this book is based, we have spent a good deal of time preparing and teaching scientific writing curricula at the University of Guam. Some of this work was supported through federal grants to the institution from the US Department of Education Title III and National Institutes of Health–National Institute for General Medical Sciences RISE Program, and we are grateful for this funding. All of the students in those classes have helped shape the way we now approach the task of guiding students through their first undergraduate biology lab report. Other important learning came from María's Master's degree in Teaching of English to Speakers of Other Languages from the University of Guam, with a thesis on students' answers to short essay questions on science exams, and her PhD in sociolinguistics from the Union Institute & University, with a dissertation on tentative language use in science. We also benefited from interaction with Mitch O'Toole, University of Newcastle, Australia, with whom María collaborated to study which language issues were particularly troubling to Pacific Island students. She is grateful for all of these opportunities, which have enriched the revision of this book.

The soil arthropod study imagined in this book is based on a project conducted by students in Lobban's Environmental Biology class at the University of Guam. We thank Dr. Tim Righetti, Cathy Nguyen, and Tina Nguyen for providing materials from a lab module on effects of pesticides on fruit flies that they developed for the Principles of Biology class at the University of Guam, on which the other model report is based.

Finally, a special thank you to Mizziel Castro for turning our sketchy ideas into professional cartoons. We appreciate her patience in revising drawings as we developed the concepts together. The painting in the "Abstract" cartoon is by James Lobban, our late father/in-law.

To the Student

Scientists Must Write

In your laboratory experiences you are apprentice scientists; scientists must share their results and conclusions with other scientists by writing papers or reports that are circulated within the research community. Without those documents, the work will not qualify as science, even if the methods met scientific criteria, because science is a collective effort to understand natural phenomena. Without "publication," people may satisfy their own curiosity but will not have contributed to that collective effort. Because reporting is key to Western science – in contrast to the way traditional knowledge is acquired and passed on – papers and reports become the credentials of scientists when they apply for jobs, promotions, or research grants. Reports are also the means for establishing accountability for research agencies and individual researchers. The centrality of reporting has been summed up in the cliché well known in academia: "publish or perish."

In the early steps as a student of biology, you will often follow a lab manual (perhaps published, perhaps prepared by your instructor) to conduct an experiment or make observations for which the outcome is already known (at least to the instructor). The purpose of the lab is to help you understand some biological process or structure and the techniques used to study it. You will then be asked to write a report of the work to demonstrate your understanding of it. In other words, the purpose is educational, not to advance science. Nevertheless, because you are repeating the work done to test a hypothesis as you learn to do science, you will be expected to write your report in a scientific format. In this handbook we walk you quickly through the steps of preparing such a report. At the end, through analysis of two published papers, we will explain the differences between a lab report and a report of work for which the purpose was to learn about nature and potentially contribute to scientific knowledge. Those reports may still be called "lab reports," but they will look different; you will use other books to teach you the fine points of preparing professional manuscripts.

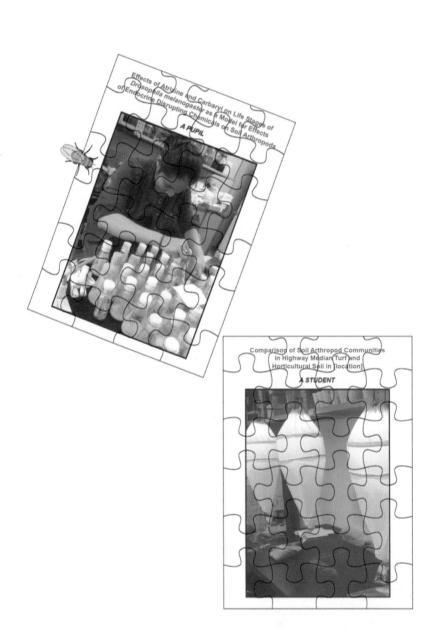

Effects of Atrizine and Carbaryl on Life Stages of *Drosophila melanogaster* as a Model for Effects of Endocrine Disrupting Chemicals on Soil Arthropods

A PUPIL

Comparison of Soil Arthropod Communities in Highway Median Turf and Horticultural Soil in [location]

A STUDENT

PART I
Introduction

1 Introduction to Science and Scientific Writing

Before getting down to the process of writing a scientific report, we want to introduce you to some ideas about science as a way of working, about the culture including the language of science. Especially important are the nature of scientific inquiry, the way that explanations depend on the question, the importance of tentative language in presenting your conclusions, and the general outline of a scientific report. We cite, using the standard author–date format, some key works by the authors who developed the ideas summarized here, and we have written more extensively about these ourselves (Lobban et al. 2014; Schefter 1996).

The Nature of Scientific Enquiry

Today, biologists understand life as a hierarchy of systems, which at each level combine to form new systems that have new properties (Mayr 1982). The levels, starting from cells (although these, too, are composed of smaller systems) are: cells, tissues, organs, body systems, individuals, populations, communities, ecosystems, and the biosphere. Some emergent properties (i.e., those that emerge when a new system is put together from component parts) are not evident from study of the parts. For example, an individual human is a system made up of a set of several interacting body systems (e.g., skeletal, muscular, vascular, nervous systems). Yet, knowing how each of these component systems functions does not allow one to predict completely how the whole human being (system) will behave. Knowing how individuals behave does not allow one to completely predict how populations (societies) will behave.

Historical components of biological and geological systems cause them to vary at every level. For example, each ecosystem is different because the species in it are the result of the history of the ecosystem; some species that could live there are not found there because some barrier prevented them getting there. Variation is one of the fundamental differences between biology and physics. Living beings are generally different from others of their species because of their genetics and environmental history. This variation must be handled by appropriate sampling and statistical methods that are part of the design of experiments or observations to test hypotheses. One cannot pick only one sample to test a hypothesis, but must replicate the test or observations; the greater the variation, the more samples are needed for statistically strong conclusions (that is, to show that the results are not due simply to chance).

All scientific studies propose and test hypotheses by seeking evidence that supports either the hypothesis or the null hypothesis, but not all involve experiments; where experiments are inappropriate or impossible, many scientific studies depend on observation and comparison (Mayr 1982; Thierry 2005).

The more familiar experimental approach requires manipulating one test condition while holding other conditions equal and including appropriate control groups. The control group allows scientists to distinguish between cause-and-effect and coincidence or chance. By using such experiments, scientists can ask questions about things happening now; these are called "proximate" questions and seek immediate causes.

When an experiment would be too large or unethical, scientists can sometimes make use of "natural experiments." Natural experiments are situations in which natural catastrophes cause changes to systems that have been studied (so that we have baseline data). For example, researchers in the Galàpagos Islands wanted to understand the mechanism by which some individuals in the marine iguana population survived better than others the famine during El Niño events (Romero & Wikelski 2010). They had concluded from previous studies that corticosterone can provide short-term behavioral and physiological benefits in coping with stresses such as famine. Their question was: Which metabolic pathway of corticosterone physiology might be the most beneficial for survival? They could not (and would not) create an experimental famine themselves, so they took baseline data on 98 individuals, which they tagged, and then waited for another El Niño event to provide the "natural experiment." After it happened, they again measured the hormone levels in the 75 survivors and were able to find out which pathway was relevant. However, while natural disasters happen frequently around the globe, they can be used as natural experiments only when they strike a population or ecosystem for which there are baseline data: The baseline is considered the experimental control.

Much medical research today depends on experiments, but medicine began with observation-and-comparison studies – descriptions of the human body, for example, and comparisons with other animals. Comparison-and-observation studies do not necessarily ask causal questions but may serve to establish patterns for which causal explanations can be sought through experiments or further observations. Moreover, experiments are never possible in studies of past phenomena or the results of historical changes, such as many biological studies in evolution and systematics and in geology. These disciplines tend to ask questions that seek causes further back; these are "evolutionary" questions. Experiments cannot address evolutionary questions because the past cannot be manipulated, but they are excellent for finding proximate causes and testing effects on organisms of conditions, drugs, pollutants, and so on. Observation-and-comparison studies can address evolutionary questions and some proximate questions.

The difference between proximate and evolutionary questions can be seen in Fig. 1.1. Many marine organisms are fluorescent when viewed in blue or UV light; this is a spectacular thing to see while diving at night, though it requires special lights and filters. A brochure for dive lights asks, "Why do organisms fluoresce?" The answer they give is that these organisms produce proteins that fluoresce when exposed to the right wavelengths of excitation light; fluorescence occurs when these proteins absorb blue light and re-emit it at visible wavelengths – "a dazzling array of greens, yellows, oranges, and reds." But this is only a partial answer, more about the *how* than the *why*, about the biochemistry of the organisms and the physics of the phenomenon. It is a proximate answer to the question and leaves us still wondering *why* these creatures fluoresce – that is, how does it help them (assuming that it does)? If we explore that question (Fig. 1.1b), we find it useful to begin with other questions, such as which organisms are fluorescent. These are proximate questions about things that are happening now, but require observation-and-comparison studies rather than experiments. These lead to other questions beyond the adaptive advantage, such as: How and when did fluorescence originate? As you can see, the answer to a question depends on what exactly

(a)

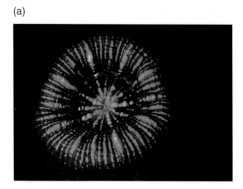

(b)

OBSERVATION & COMPARISON   **EXPERIMENTS**

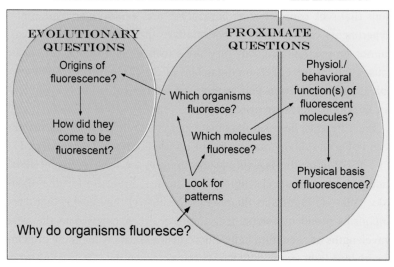

Figure 1.1 (a) Green and red fluorescence in a sea anemone, taken underwater at night in Okinawa. [Photo credit: Shawn M. Miller, okinawanaturephotography.com] (b) Possible series of questions related to "Why do organisms fluoresce?" Traced from that starting point, questions lead first into observation and comparison studies to find patterns and establish what needs to be explained, then go into experimental studies to seek answers to physiological/behavioral and physicochemical questions. The smaller circle encloses evolutionary ("ultimate") questions, which have some historical component. The larger circle encloses proximate questions, which can be addressed entirely by what goes on here and now. The two rectangles enclose the two approaches to gaining knowledge: observation-and-comparison and experimentation.

the question means, and this leads us to explore explanations in science further, since you will have to explain things in your lab report.

Explanations are Central to Science but Not Always Easy to Write

Explanation is central to scientific writing. In science we describe natural phenomena and then we explain them (Love 1996). Explanations typically involve statements of cause and effect, and it is the task of science to separate causal relationships, correlations, and coincidences. "Why" questions expect "because" answers; that is, a description of a cause-and-effect relationship. In research reports, explanations most often appear in the Discussion section, where the results are interpreted.

It is not immediately obvious what constitutes a satisfactory explanation, because questions are often ambiguous. For example, while "Because of gravity" might be a satisfactory explanation of the observation that things that are dropped will fall, "because of pollution" would not be a satisfactory explanation of why there was a change in populations of light and dark peppered moths when the Industrial Revolution in Britain blackened trees (Fig. 1.2) (Love 1996). This explanation would need to include how the moth is camouflaged from predatory birds, the variation in colors in moth offspring from light to dark, and the selection pressure gradually favoring darker moths. The difference lies partly in how much knowledge the reader can be expected to have, and partly in how directly the cause is connected to the event effect. Gravity is the direct cause of objects falling toward the ground, and this relationship is simple, direct, and widely known. In explaining the peppered moth colors, however, there are several problems: First, knowledge of the underlying mechanism (in this case selective predation) cannot be assumed. Second, pollution does not directly cause the change in peppered moth populations; rather, there is a chain of events: pollution → black trees → lighter moths being more visible to predators → population changes from mostly light to mostly dark moths. Third, part of the explanation involves proximate questions (pollution) and part involves evolutionary questions (adaptation) (Hannam & Rutowski n.d.). Appropriate explanations depend on the exact question being asked; as in Fig. 1.1, "Why do organisms fluoresce?" can be explained in many ways.

Figure 1.2 Peppered moths, light and dark phase on a dark tree in the United Kingdom. © John Mason/ardea.com

In scientific reports you are often faced with explaining discrepancies in data. You will often have to explain differences between your own findings, from a given location under certain conditions, with the relevant literature from other places and other conditions. You will use the literature by analogy, recognizing that the more dissimilar the places or conditions were, the weaker the analogy. In these cases you often have to try to sort out how the different conditions will affect the applicability of particular conclusions. That is, you have to explain why certain conclusions can be applied for comparison, whereas others cannot.

Biological Conclusions Must be Expressed in Tentative Language

As a result of variation in biological materials, biologists do not formulate laws that are invariably true, but we seek principles that apply with more or less certainty. Uncertainty is inevitable in biology and in most other sciences – apart from physics and chemistry – and thus while results can sometimes be expressed statistically, conclusions generally cannot. Scientists must express their level of confidence in their conclusions when they write reports and papers. They use **tentative language** ("hedging") to do this (Halliday & Martin 1993; Hyland 1998; Lemke 1990). Unfortunately, these words are often stripped away in media reports, so that the general public is unaware of them and may even think that using such words is a sign that the scientist is unreliable. In fact, the opposite is true: Claims without tentative language should not be trusted. There is always uncertainty in scientific conclusions, and as an apprentice scientist you must learn how to express your confidence in the conclusions you claim in your reports.

Tentative language ranges from words such as "may," "could," and "probably," to phrases that incorporate verbs such as "suggest," "appear," and "expect." For example, in the reports of the International Panel on Climate Change, there are many conclusions with different confidence levels, and it is essential for people and policymakers to understand the differences. So, a set of terms was defined and used consistently (Table 1.1). Different terms have different relative strength – "probable" is stronger than "possible." Notice how tentative language is used in this excerpt from one of the scientific papers analyzed in Chapter 10 (Palacios-Vargas et al. 2007), where the authors explicitly address their confidence in their conclusion. The tentative language expressions are: "possible," "could be considered," and "remains limited."

Table 1.1 Definitions of confidence terms used in the International Panel on Climate Change reports starting in 2002

Virtually certain > 99% probability of occurrence
Extremely likely > 95%
Very likely > 90%
Likely > 66%
More likely than not > 50%
Unlikely < 33%
Very unlikely < 10%
Extremely unlikely < 5%

> Overall, our density Arthropoda values are higher than those recorded in a humid tropical forest, but lower than those found in temperate ecosystems (Haarlow 1960; Lebrun 1971). Therefore, it is possible that the tropical dry forest ecosystem could be considered an intermediate condition regarding soil arthropods total density. However, the level of confidence for this assertion remains limited by the small number of studies with complete estimates of soil arthropods density and composition in forest ecosystems.

There are Several Writing Genres within a Scientific Paper

Scientific papers contain four main sections that are written in different styles or *genres* (Hyland 2004; Swales 1990, 2004). The Introduction and the Discussion are both written as logical arguments; the Introduction presents the rationale for the study and the particular objectives, hypotheses, or research questions; the Discussion explains how well the data support the hypotheses. Methods and Results, however, are written in narrative form, specifying in logical order what was done and what was found. The details of how to write each section form the bulk of Part II of this handbook.

PART II
Writing the First Draft
Format

2 Starting to Write

Facing the Task

Our goal is to start you writing *science*. *Writing Undergraduate Lab Reports* will help you to develop the specific skills you need from your general background in writing; it bridges the gap between the many books about writing term papers and the advanced books about writing papers for publication in scientific journals. Neither of those groups of books is appropriate for science lab reports based on a lab manual. The chapters in Part II of this handbook can be used as a step-by-step guide as you draft your first report, by walking you through the structure of a report. Part III shows you how to revise your paper and refine your scientific style; these are skills you will continue to practice as you write more reports.

No matter whether your research went smoothly or seemed chaotic, you can write a good report. Your grade will probably depend on how well you show that you understand the work and how well you write your report using scientific format and style. Ask! As you organize your thoughts and data for the report and write simple, clear sentences, you will come to a clearer understanding of the study.

> Writing a science lab report is not difficult,
> but it is not an English composition.

We assume that in conducting your work you followed either a published laboratory manual or an unpublished set of instructions from your professor, and that these will tell you what to include in your report, how to analyze the data to prepare appropriate graphs and tables, and give you a start on the background of the study. That guidance about the content of the report goes hand-in-hand with this book, which shows you the **format**. Both sets of instructions should be beside you, together with your notes and results, as you begin to write.

Writing for Science Classes

A lab report is neither a term paper nor a scientific paper. You do not have to read and summarize a large number of books and papers; your report needs only a small amount of relevant background information to give context to your own experiments or observations. Yet, while a lab report must have the structure of a scientific paper, it has a different audience and purpose. A scientific paper is written to fellow scientists to present and discuss new information and ideas. Your lab report is written to your professor, who is already familiar with the work, to show that you understand the process and significance of the study.

Good scientific writing is not literary, in spite of the fact that scientists use "literature" as a generic term for their writings. You do not have to be a masterful creative writer to write an excellent lab report! Rather, you need to use straightforward words and clear sentences that unambiguously convey your meaning. The format of a scientific paper already gives you a broad outline for your report that should get you past the writer's block that can come from staring at a blank page with no idea of what to write.

Structure: The IMRAD Formula

The plan of a scientific paper, and so of your report, is this:

> Title and author(s)
> [Abstract]
> Introduction
> Materials and methods
> Results
> Discussion
> References (or literature cited)
> Figures and tables

The core of this plan is Introduction, Methods, Results, and Discussion, known as IMRAD by those who use acronyms. This structure changed the more narrative style of the nineteenth century because it helps busy readers find the information they want.

Read all instructions from your professor!

While the overall IMRAD plan is generally agreed on, scientific writing style is to some extent a matter of individual choice, with accepted criteria within each discipline that you will gradually master. Find out what your professor wants (e.g., by reading the course syllabus). We will indicate by Ask! in the following chapters where there are divergent opinions on points of style.

The fact that a paper is presented in the order given above does not mean that you have to write it in that order. In fact, if you have difficulty starting with the Introduction, we recommend that you try starting with the Methods. The Introduction may be more difficult to write because there are more ways to structure it. The Methods section consists simply of a factual narrative of what you did. You can use the next few chapters in whatever order you need, but we suggest you read the whole of Part II – on writing the first draft – to get an overview of what you'll be doing. Then re-read each chapter before you begin to write that section. Also, outlining each of your sections will help you to organize your ideas. Writing a lab report is like putting together a jigsaw puzzle: You have to put all the facts and ideas in order so that they make a clear picture. Use the outlining features of the software you are using and set up the main headings as given above.

The outline will make it easier for you to write the report – because you can first note down the points to cover – and easier for the reader to follow it. Start by creating topic sentences that give the key points to be made (Fig. 2.1); each will likely be expanded into a paragraph. While the report is at this stage you can easily glance over the key points. Later, you can collapse the outline to show just the first (topic) sentence to again easily review it all for a sense of the logical flow. Of course, this process is not unique to science writing. You may change the order as you write or when you revise, so there is no need to strive for perfection now. Just get started!

▭ Title and Authors

▭ [Abstract]

✚ Introduction
  ▫ Connect to something important
  ▫ Introduce the process
  ▫ Introduce the organism(s)
  ▫ Introduce the equipment
  ▫ State the objective(s)

▭ Materials and Methods

▭ Results

▭ Discussion

▭ References (or Literature Cited)

▭ Tables and Figures

Figure 2.1 First stages of a lab report document in outline view, showing the main headings and the sequence of paragraphs in the Introduction (in this generic example we have only stated the topics, in future specific examples we give draft topic sentences).

3 Introduction

Purpose of the Introduction

The Introduction gives the background to the work, starting with the broad context of the study and leading up to the objective(s). In published papers it gives the reader the background needed to understand the context and relevance of the work. For you, it serves to show the instructor that you understand the context and relevance of the study. One way of thinking about the Introduction is as a series of questions relating to the rationale for the study:

- How is the organism or process important?
- Why was this organism chosen? (Convenient to handle? Important organism? Good model system for the process under study?)
- What methods are available for this study?
- Why was your particular method chosen?
- What is known about the process, especially in this organism?
- What was the hypothesis or question being addressed?

Writing the Introduction

For a skillful Introduction, you need to choose relevant and correct information from the scientific literature, paraphrase it, and reassemble it into your own logical sequence, citing the sources to support each statement (see Fig. 3.1). Do not use your lab manual as the sole source! Consult your textbook and any references it suggests, or any texts your professor has put on reserve for you. For a report on a single lab you may not need to go further. Ask! Students often ask how long the

Introduction should be. The answer is: As long as it needs to be, given the content that is needed and your goal to demonstrate your understanding, but usually 1–3 pages of double-spaced typescript.

Every statement you make that is drawn from someone else's work needs a reference to the source. If you have several ideas together from one source, you need to cite the source only once. However, some things are so well known that no citation is necessary (e.g., "Plants are photosynthetic"); your opening sentence might be sufficiently general (see the second paper in Chapter 10). If in doubt, cite a source. As you write, cite sources in author–date format for all the statements you make, and notice that a parenthetic citation at the end of a sentence goes *before* the period (full stop), not after it.

> Correct: experimental conditions (Romero et al. 2000).
> Incorrect: experimental conditions. (Romero et al. 2000)

Be sure to keep careful track of your references! Add each reference to the References section as soon as you add a citation. You can put references in order and the proper style when you have finished writing your text (see Chapter 9). You can read more about citations below, but first we want to finish showing you the content and structure of the Introduction. The content outline of the Introduction was shown in Fig. 2.1 and two specific examples are given at the end of this chapter.

> Start broadly, then narrow down to your objectives.

Begin by putting the reader in the picture with a statement that links what you are doing to something of established importance. You will be able to get good ideas for opening lines by looking at the opening lines of the papers and book chapters you have been referred to, or from the treatment of the topic in the lab manual or textbook. For our two main examples, we might point out the importance of soil arthropods, or note the pervasive effects of endocrine-disrupting chemicals (EDCs) on non-target species, including humans:

> Soil arthropods play major ecological roles including shredding organic matter, recycling nutrients to support plant growth, and protecting plants from predators and parasites (Menta 2012).

> Numerous endocrine-disrupting chemicals (EDCs) in the environment are pesticides that do not just target the intended pests but also upset the hormonal balance of wildlife species and humans that are inadvertently exposed to them (Mnif et al. 2011).

This first statement, linking the study to something the reader should see as important, is called the centrality statement; it may need developing into a short paragraph. For now, do not worry about making it great, and if you cannot come up with anything quickly, just write "Centrality statement?!" in your outline and try the next paragraph. Next, decide what items need to be introduced; depending on your particular study this may include saying something about the organism(s) or habitat involved, the equipment or technique used, and the process under study.

Each topic should get a separate paragraph with a clear topic sentence first (we will say more about this when you have a draft to revise; Chapter 8). For now, try to keep the connections between sentences in a paragraph by following the advice of Gopen and Swan (1990), who explored "topic" and "stress" *parts of a sentence*. The first *part of a sentence* (the topic position) should include a word or phrase linking back to the previous sentence to set the context for the new material (as here in the words italicized). The new material goes in the second part of the sentence, the stress position. If you cannot see the links between sentences, your reader will probably also miss them. It is better to write clearly from the start than to try to sort out a muddled mess during revision! Also pay attention to "signpost" words that tell the reader – and you – where you are going, such as: first, second, however, although, on the other hand, for example.

The order of the paragraphs should follow logically from the opening paragraph (Fig. 3.1), and should lead naturally to the final paragraph of the Introduction, the statement of objectives. There should be something in the opening lines to indicate what things are to be introduced, and we will then expect a paragraph about each, or there should be a connection between the end of one paragraph and the beginning of the next.

End your Introduction by saying what the purpose of your work was. You may be required to write out formal hypotheses or it may be sufficient to state the question that you addressed in the lab. Never write that the objective was to "learn the technique" or "to measure this or that."

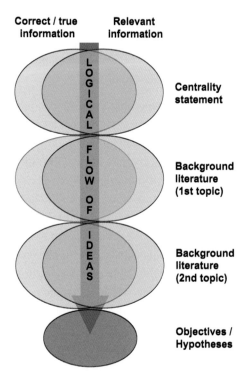

Correct / true   **Relevant**
Information   **Information**

L
O
G
I
C
A
L   **Centrality**
                         statement

F
L
O
W   **Background**
                         literature
O   **(1st topic)**
F

I
D
E   **Background**
A   **literature**
S   **(2nd topic)**

                         Objectives /
                         Hypotheses

Figure 3.1 The quality of your Introduction depends on having correct and relevant information organized into a flow starting from the centrality statement and ending with the objectives.

Whatever pedagogical purpose the professor may have had in assigning this lab, you are writing up the test of a hypothesis, not the goals of the course.

The Model Reports

Throughout the rest of these chapters we will develop two model lab reports to illustrate the process. Both are fictitious, although based loosely on actual student projects. The first of these is an observational study of soil arthropods using Berlese funnels, the second an experimental study of the effect of EDCs on fruit fly larvae. If you would like an overview, the abstracts of the reports are given in Chapter 7.

Our Introduction outline (topic sentences) for the report on the use of Berlese funnels might look like this (the citations are real papers and the references are listed in Chapter 9):

⊕ Introduction
- Soil arthropods play major ecological roles including shredding organic matter, recycling nutrients to support plant growth, and protecting plants from predators and parasites (Menta 2012).
- Arthropods include insects, spiders, mites, collembolids, and other groups. … The most abundant in soils are mites and collembolids, which typically are about 60% and 40% respectively of the total arthropods (Menta 2012). …
- Agricultural soils have lower diversity than undisturbed fields or natural habitats because of frequent disturbance and application of chemicals (Desmond & Alex 2013).
- Soil arthropods can be extracted from soil by several techniques, each with advantages and disadvantages (Barberena-Arias et al. 2012). … The Berlese funnel is the most commonly used; it consists of….
- There has been little study of soil arthropods in turfgrass (Rochefort et al. 2006)
- The objective of the study was to determine the arthropod community structure of two urban sites, the grass median strip of a main road and the intensely cultivated soil in an organic community garden.

Our Introduction outline (topic sentences) for the EDCs study might look like this:

⊕ Introduction
- Numerous endocrine-disrupting chemicals (EDCs) in the environment are pesticides that do not just target the intended pests but also upset the hormonal balance of wildlife species and humans that are inadvertently exposed to them (Mnif et al. 2011).
- Atrazine is a widely used broad-leaf weed killer (herbicide) and carbaryl is a popular insecticide. …
- Soil arthropods (insects and related organisms) are generally beneficial in the soil (Menta 2012) and are not the intended targets of agricultural insecticides…. Soil arthropods are not easy to rear in captivity but the common fruit fly, *Drosophila melanogaster*, can serve as a model organism.
- The objective of this study was to test the effects of various concentrations of the herbicide atrazine on larval development in the fruit fly, and to compare these with effects of the insecticide carbaryl.

Citing Scientific Literature

Scientists pride themselves on making discoveries – discovery is the essence of science – so giving credit to other people when you incorporate their findings into your own writing is very important. It is the Critical Thinking standard of Fairness (Paul & Elder n.d.). Scandals and lawsuits have resulted when one scientist appeared to adopt the work of another as his own. Taking other people's work without giving credit is plagiarism, a most serious academic offense because it is stealing of others' ideas, words, or other intellectual property. Your name on the paper implies that the thoughts, facts, and words are your own unless you say otherwise. Another good reason to cite is that literature citations make your report look more scholarly.

There is rarely reason to quote from scientific writing, because the writing is secondary to the information and not literary, so you must paraphrase the original – rewrite it in your own words (this requires that you understand what you are reading!). Particularly in science writing, it is important not to change the evidence or conclusions you are referencing, so in paraphrasing the words of others you must not change the information by the way you change the words. It is important not to misrepresent the earlier studies by overstating the conclusions, or by changing the degree of confidence in the conclusions (detailed guidelines for science are given by Roig 2015). Sometimes short, simple statements cannot be changed much. For instance, in referring to Romero and Wikelski's (2010) paper in Chapter 1, we adapted their statement:

> Corticosterone can provide short-term behavioural (Wingfield & Romero 2001) and physiological (Sapolsky et al. 2000) benefits in coping with stressors, including stressors consisting of worsening environmental conditions (e.g. Romero et al. 2000).

to say:

> ... (Romero & Wikelski 2010). They knew from previous studies that corticosterone can provide short-term behavioral and physiological benefits in coping with stresses such as famine.

What do you do about "second-hand" references? When you read textbooks, you will find that most of the facts and ideas there are credited to someone else. Who do you cite? For your report, cite only the books or papers that you see. You can assume that these published works are authoritative and you can cite them as your sources. Do not include in your reference list works you have not actually consulted.

Do not put references in footnotes; collect them in the References section. Whereas footnotes are common in the humanities, they are unacceptable in science reports. (Footnotes are not used for parenthetic comments, either. Such asides are simply written in parentheses, like this.) However, in published papers there may be a cluster of footnotes on the first page, giving authors' affiliations/addresses, dates the manuscript was received and accepted, or a list of abbreviations. You won't need any footnotes in the text.

The Hypotheses

The objectives statement in the Introduction is often broader than a hypothesis, and may cover several hypotheses. For example, the objective might be "to test the effect of temperature on respiration of" some organism or tissue. A hypothesis is a formal statement of a question about nature that can be tested. Following that example, it would be: "Respiration rate of ... is affected by (is a function of) temperature." There is a null hypothesis, the opposite, which in this case is: "Respiration of ... is not a function of temperature." Or, an ecological example: "The distribution of organism X on the seashore is (or is not) related to distance above low tide level." In the sort of lab exercises you are doing now, the hypotheses will have already been tested, perhaps many times in many organisms, and the lab manual may well tell you what to expect; you are not in a process of discovery. Yet, in doing it again to learn how, you are following the same steps and you should be able to write out what hypotheses you were testing.

There are always hypotheses.

Even if the hypotheses are not clear in the lab manual or from what the professor has told you, there is at least one hypothesis, and you must find out or figure out what it is. People used to think that it would be better to observe with no preconceptions of what you would find, but in fact there can be no science without hypotheses. The whole point of the experiment or observations is to provide data with which to assess the hypothesis versus the null hypothesis. Charles Darwin once wrote that one "might as well go into a gravel pit and count the pebbles and describe the colors. How odd it is that anyone should not see that observation must be for or against some view if it is to be of any service" (Darwin 1903, Vol. 1, p. 195; see also Ayala 2009). Likewise, observation-and-comparison studies are also all based on hypotheses. For example, a lab on chromatography of plant pigments (re)tests the hypothesis that the chosen plant has chlorophyll a and b, etc. (or some other combination of pigments). Even a taxonomic question, such as identifying a species, has hypotheses ("This specimen matches the description – has all the characters – of *Genus X species y*," or it does not). When you understand the study, you will know what the hypotheses are. Conversely, if you cannot state the question clearly, you will be unable to answer it; this will indicate to the professor that you do not understand the exercise. Remember that one of the goals of writing up the lab work is to bring you to a clear understanding.

Let's look at the hypotheses behind the objectives in the two sample lab reports we are developing.

Underlying the objective of the soil arthropods study ("to determine the arthropod community structure of two urban sites, the grass median strip of a main road and the intensely cultivated soil in a community garden") are several possible hypotheses. One is that the two urban sites will have different arthropod communities (or not). A second could be that communities in the grass strips will be similar to (or differ from) communities described in published papers about turfgrass communities. We would not consider as hypotheses questions about factors influencing the soil communities (such as heavier hydrocarbon loads in the median strip) unless we were going to measure those factors and thereby test the hypotheses (as was done in the published paper we show in Chapter 10). However, one can *propose* these hypotheses in the Discussion when explaining differences.

Underlying the objective of the EDCs study ("to test the effects of various concentrations of the herbicide atrazine on larval development in the fruit fly, and to compare these with effects of the insecticide carbaryl") are the following hypotheses, among others: (1) sub-lethal doses of either pesticide will alter (or not) the development and/or survival of the fruit fly larvae; (2) the herbicide will have effects at higher (or equal, or lower) doses than the insecticide; (3) there will be synergistic effects when both pesticides are present; (4) the effects of either pesticide will be similar (or not) to data in the literature for other insects tested with the same chemicals under similar conditions.

4 Materials and Methods

This chapter specifies what materials you used and how you used them. It is one of the easiest to write, especially if you already have a set of procedures written for you. In chemistry it is often called "Experimental." Ask!

If you have never written a science lab report before, you might write a narrative about your adventures in the lab or field, instead of giving a concise account of the materials and the methods. You might also try to follow the format of a lab manual with a list of materials and a numbered set of steps. Neither is appropriate for a report in a scientific format.

If you exactly followed a set of written instructions and you are not required to write out the full procedure, you may state briefly what was done and cite the manual Ask!:

> Photosynthesis of spinach chloroplasts (*Spinacia oleracea*) was measured in a Gilson respirometer, using the procedure in Author (date).

More likely you didn't exactly follow the written procedures, especially if you used a published lab manual, because your professor probably adapted it in some way, such as by using a different organism or slightly different apparatus. We assume here that you will be required to write out the details of the materials and methods.

You do not need to include every little detail, but you must decide which details you need. In a published paper, the methods need to have enough detail so that another scientist in the same field of study could repeat the work and assess the validity of the results and conclusions. Your report is not intended to show the professor how to do it, of course – she told *you* how to do it! – but to show her that you understood what you were doing, did it right, and noted any deviations – and that you can write in the scientific style.

As usual, start with an outline. You may need to answer questions such as:

- What organism was used? (Give species name, phenotype, culture, or strain number as appropriate.)
- What parts of the organism, and if removed, how? If cultures, how much or how dense?
- How many replicates?
- If in the field, where was the study site? (At least give coordinates from GPS; a map and/or photo may be appropriate.)
- How big was the sample size? How were organisms harvested, weighed, etc.?
- What apparatus or equipment was used? (A diagram or photo might be appropriate.)
- What were the experimental conditions (temperature, light, medium, etc., as appropriate)?
- What chemicals were used in the experimental treatments?
- If part of the professor's purpose in this lab is for you to learn to use particular equipment, you should give enough detail to show you used it correctly (calibration etc.)
- What was the composition of the reaction mixture (if any)?
- How long were the treatments?
- What were the controls (see Fig. 4.2)?
- How were data handled (calculations, statistical tests)?

Remember that you are writing the report to your professor, not providing a set of instructions to another student. You can leave out certain steps as obvious (e.g., that the test tubes were clean, or that when you added flies to the vial you took out the stopper and then put it back). You do not need to mention whether you used a marker pen to label collecting bags or experimental vials. Your lab manual may include such details for your benefit, but you do not need to repeat them in your report.

The main thing you will need to do with lab manual instructions is to recast them from present imperative ("Do this, do that") into past tense ("This was done, we did that"). The work is over and is written up in the past tense. Also, don't overuse "then." If you write out a series of steps, the reader will assume they were in that order (therefore put them in order!). "Then" is okay now and then.

Let's follow our two sample lab reports to see what questions we need to cover, and how the outline might look.

For the soil arthropods study, we need to begin with a description of the study sites, which should include the GPS coordinates and perhaps be accompanied by a map; depending on circumstances, photos of each site might be useful. Then the collection should be described, including the date, the method of choosing representative samples, the number of samples, and so on, and how the samples were handled before they were placed in the funnels. If you were following a published source, or your protocol was based on one, the reference should be cited. The extraction procedure with the Berlese funnels needs to be described, and a diagram or photograph would be helpful, especially if the funnels were homemade (Fig. 4.1). The strength of the light bulb and the time of exposure are important considerations in the success of the extraction of organisms and must be specified (again a reference is appropriate). The means of identifying the different arthropods should be given (references to books/ websites), and mention made of whether the animals were photographed

Figure 4.1 Sample figures for the Methods section. Captions in the report (numbered assuming map = Fig. 1): "Fig. 2. Photo of median strip study site at (street, city) showing approximate locations of samples. Fig. 3. Berlese funnels in use. Funnel consists of a wire mesh pan to hold the sample, covered by canvas with a light inside, and a funnel below the pan to direct arthropods into the trap (a plastic bag containing 95% ethanol as preservative)."

Carbaryl concentration (ppm)	Atrazine concentration (ppm)			
	0	0.4	4	40
0	Double control	Carbaryl control	Carbaryl control	Carbaryl control
0.4	Atrazine control	Test	Test	Test
4	Atrazine control	Test	Test	Test
40	Atrazine control	Test	Test	Test

Figure 4.2 Matrix diagram of the experimental design. Caption in report: "Fig. 1. Experimental design of the pesticides tests."

for documentation or retained as voucher specimens. Any diversity indices should be specified (give the formula and the reference for the method) and briefly say what the indices measure and why they were used rather than others. Also note any other statistical treatments used in analyzing the raw data, but you don't need to say that you made graphs of the data.

For the pesticides study, the Methods section would begin with the organism under study – species name, and the method for establishing subcultures and raising the larvae. What stages were counted (larvae, pupae, adults?) and how often? Then the pesticides need to be listed along with the brand and any relevant formulation details from the packaging, and the method of preparing the contaminated growth media. Say what dosages were used and what the control was; in this case a figure showing the matrix of treatments might help clarify the combinations of pesticides (Fig. 4.2). The text might then read: "A series of four concentrations of atrazine was prepared for each of four concentrations of carbaryl (Figure 1)." State how the data were analyzed (e.g., by creating pivot tables).

Tables and Figures

Although most of your tables and figures may be in the Results section, you can see that you may well have some in the Materials and Methods. All should be placed in the manuscript after all the other text (that is, after the References), on separate pages, each with a caption that explains what the table or figure shows. The caption must also explain any symbols or abbreviations used. Do not use the chart title feature of spreadsheet programs, but do make sure both axes are labeled in graphs. Number all tables consecutively (Table 1, Table 2, etc.) and figures with their own consecutive series of numbers. Note that unlike a book with chapters, where figures are numbered 1.1, 1.2, etc., in a lab report or scientific article they are just numbered 1, 2, etc. Table captions are placed above the table, with any explanation of notes placed below the table. Figure captions go below the picture. Study the examples in this chapter and Chapter 5, and in the sample published papers in Chapter 10.

"Garbage in, Garbage out"

5 Results

Before you can write the Results section you must create the graphs and tables from the numerical data you recorded and do any calculations necessary, following your professor's instructions. Here we will tell you what to say about the results, because this section must have text – you cannot just insert the tables and graphs! But as you create your graphs and tables, check for errors – both before, by checking the data records, and when you see the first graphs, which can serve as a check. Any errors that cannot be corrected must be addressed in the Discussion, but errors that can be corrected should be corrected.

Sources of Error

Discovering the sources of error is like troubleshooting a machine or a computer program, except that in your undergraduate lab you probably cannot go back to the experiment, make adjustments, and try again. You are analyzing after the fact.

Here are some potential sources of error:

Procedural Errors. These are mistakes in technique, such as adding a bit more or less of a test solution; or accidentally losing some biomass during dry weight measurements. Such errors will displace the data point along one or the other axis of a graph. No matter how precise you think you were, there will always be some variation. There's little you can do about these errors after the fact. Obviously, if you know that you lost half of your sample or added 30 percent more reagent, you should disregard the data from it. More likely, you will not have noticed the slip, or the error was not that great, and you must include it and explain in the Discussion.

Errors in Measurements or Observations. It is easy to misread an instrument, especially if it has an analog read-out. When the value is changing with time, you have to try to pick a value and simultaneously note the time. You can easily be off by a bit. Also, you may have introduced some unnoticed bias. In the absence of instrument readings, different observers may score differently: In our soil arthropod study, some students may underestimate one type of organism and overestimate another if they fail to distinguish between them. In this exercise, 30–35 percent of the arthropod specimens could not be identified (because of our inexperience with arthropod taxonomy), and it is also possible that we misidentified some of the smaller, less distinctive forms.

Errors in Recording or Recopying. Look for possibilities of misread or miscopied numbers. If you have had to copy data, e.g., from a handwritten sheet into an electronic worksheet, it is possible to have transposed digits (this will affect only one datum), or skipped a reading (this could affect all subsequent entries). Occasionally the error may be big enough that you can spot it – but you may not be able to fix it. For instance, a pH of 41 is impossible. But was it really 14 or 4.1? If you can't be absolutely sure, don't guess. Guessing can only make things worse, and puts you at risk of falsifying data. You can reduce this source of error by developing the habit of checking numbers at the time you record them. Also recheck when you copy from your lab notes onto tables and graphs. Be especially careful when copying columns or rows of numbers as it is easy to skip a line, then all the subsequent data are misaligned. Checking is essential, because in spite of the adage "garbage in, garbage out," it is possible to enter erroneous data and get a result that doesn't look like garbage, even though it is erroneous.

Errors in Computation. Check your calculations; cross-check if possible. Don't assume that your classmates had it right if your answer is different – you may have the correct answer! Go back to the raw data if you need to. Common errors in computation include misplacing a decimal, especially when converting between units (e.g., milligrams to micrograms). Make sure your units are consistent. Compare your results with expected values to see if you are close (but be aware that there may be other reasons why your results are not as expected).

Writing the Results

The purpose of the Results section is to present your findings with the supporting evidence. Thus, each paragraph should start with a topic sentence that makes a claim for the result; for example: "Photosynthesis was saturated at a light intensity of 450 μmol m^{-2} s^{-1} (Figure 1)." The figure or table with the data to support the claim is written in parentheses at the end of the sentence. Graphs and tables present data, they do not state results. They are the evidence, the statements are conclusions based on the evidence – not proof.

You must make some statements about your results.

Start with the most important result if you have several. Use the past tense throughout, because it is what you found. Avoid starting sentences by referring to a figure or table ("Figure 1 shows ... "); the purpose is not to describe them, and doing so will distract from focusing on the findings.

Simple data, such as percentage composition, can sometimes be stated simply in a sentence rather than presented in a table. This takes up much less space and is easier for you to do. Ask! For instance, "Cell dry matter was 20% protein, 10% fat, 30% carbohydrate, and 40% ash." If you have more data – the compositions of five species, for instance – make a table. Do not give data in both a table and a sentence.

The Results should state only what you found.

Give only your results. "Your" in this context means you and your lab partner, if any, or even the whole class if the collective data are in your report.

Keep comments on the results for the Discussion section. In the Results section, simply state the claims and refer to the evidence. There should not be any references to other works (published data or statements of theory); this would indicate that you are saying things that should be in the Discussion. The place for comparing your data with theory and for interpreting them is in the Discussion. If, on the other hand, you later find yourself introducing results in the Discussion or discussing results that you neglected to present, go back and insert the data into the Results section.

As you write, continue numbering your graphs (and any drawings such as maps or apparatus) as figures, in the order in which you refer to them. Number the tables, in order, with a separate series of numbers. Remember that the figures and tables are usually placed at the end of a manuscript report, not inserted into the text. Ask!

Here are examples of results statements from each hypothetical study and the evidence they refer to (Figs. 5.1 and 5.2; Table 5.1). You can see samples of published graphs and tables in the annotated articles in Chapter 10.

From the pesticides report:

> Increasing concentrations of the herbicide atrazine reduced the number of flies produced; at the highest concentration it was as toxic as the highest dose of the insecticide carbaryl (Fig. 3).

From the soil report:

> Six major categories of arthropods were identified in the soil samples (Table 1); of these, mites (Fig. 4) and collembolids were the most abundant at both sites.

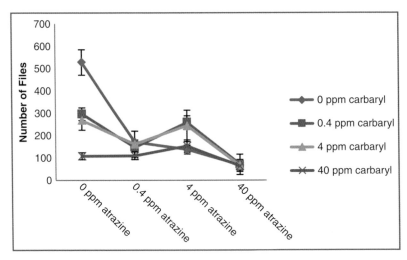

Figure 5.1 Example of a well-designed graph from the pesticides study. Caption in report: "Figure 3. The number of flies (adults) produced at 4 doses of atrazine at each of 4 doses of carbaryl."

Table 5.1 Example of a clear and simple table from the soil study. Notice how footnotes are used for any notes in a table. Caption in report: "Table 1. Percent composition of arthropod taxa in the two soils (number in taxon out of total individuals, all three samples)."

Arthropod taxa	Median strip soil	Garden soil
Acari (mites)	34	25
Collembola	15	21
Formicidae (ants)	11	20
Diplopoda (millipedes)	5	3
Pseudoscorpionida	0	1
Curculionoidea (weevils)	0	<1[a]
Unidentified	35	30

[a]A single weevil was identified (Fig. 4).

Figure 5.2 Results figure for the soil study. Caption in report: "Figure 4. Several types of arthropod from the garden soil sample, photographed against a 1-cm section of a ruler, using a smartphone and clip-on magnifier. A = ants; M = mites; W = weevil; U = unidentified. Scale bar = 1 mm."

6 Discussion

The Discussion answers the overall question: What do the results mean? It is essentially an argument in support of your conclusions about the hypotheses, based on the results. It must include both the limitations of your study and any sources of error – both limit the strength of your conclusions – and a comparison of your results to the literature (or expected findings). It also shows that you understand and can apply the principles of the system under study and the instruments used. You must also answer any questions your instructor posed to help you understand the lab work. The structure of the Discussion is much less prescriptive than for other sections, but you might organize the Discussion around a number of smaller questions:

1. What is your interpretation of the results, in light of the hypotheses or research question and the published literature?
2. What are the significant sources of error in the results? (How accurate and how reliable were your results?)
3. Do the results support the hypothesis or the null hypothesis? (Or perhaps neither or both?)
4. What changes in procedure would give better results and/or what additional experiments would help distinguish between the hypotheses?

Whether your experiment worked as planned or deteriorated into chaos, you can write a good report. The key section in the report is the Discussion, because it is where you show that you understand what should have happened and what did happen. Do not blame yourself or others for what went wrong. Simply consider the sources of error and the extent to which they affect the data.

Accounting for errors is not about assigning blame.

We suggest you start the Discussion by considering the strengths of your data. Highlight the main finding, or write a one-sentence summary of the results. Only then describe the sources of error and discuss the reliability of the results.

The assessment of reliability is best handled in two parts: First, deal with any errors in the data or observations that you were unable to correct (see Chapter 5) and any deviations from the established procedures that might have affected the results. Any differences in the procedures, whether intentional or inadvertent, by the professor or you, have the potential to create differences in the results compared with expectations. Look over your Materials and Methods section and lab notes to see what changes there were. Consider the consequences of the errors and changes; explain what effect each might have had. Not all errors have equal impact – some may be trivial, within the range of error expected in your process, others may seriously limit the conclusions you can draw about the hypothesis.

Second, discuss the limitations of the study and the impact these have on the accuracy of the results and the extent to which the results can be applied in general. Limitations are constraints built into the work by the time and resources available. Even in the real world of research, the most common limitation in scientific studies is the amount of data, because there is often insufficient time or funding to carry out the ideal amount of sampling or replication. There are also limitations and sometimes biases in the equipment/procedures used that especially affect comparisons with studies done using different methods. For example, Berlese funnels have well-known biases. Suppose that a certain group of arthropods has low numbers in your sample, compared to expected values – could it be that there is some bias in the sampling (ranging from collecting the soil to what organisms come out of the soil in the funnels) that could have limited the collection of that group more than others? In your undergraduate lab day, these constraints are much more severe; it may be that results will not be as clear as expected because of variation and that more data are needed to improve the results.

The number of samples is often too small for the variation present, but before calling for more repetitions of the same, you must assess the quality of the data you have, particularly to see if there are causes of variation that could have been reduced. This is where you are particularly able to show the instructor that you understand the process and procedures.

If necessary, you should freely admit a failure to get useful results; show that you understand what might have gone wrong. Notice that there is an important difference between negative results and a failure to get results. If you are following a lab manual, you can be fairly sure that the principle you have been given to demonstrate is a well-established hypothesis, so if your results don't demonstrate it, something went wrong – that is, you failed to get results. You could report that you were unable to show a relationship between respiration rate and temperature; you could not conclude that there was no relationship between respiration rate and temperature.

The point of examining the errors is only to evaluate the results. Do not assign blame or take on any for yourself, even if you or your lab partner did something really stupid! Give a nonjudgmental scientific explanation.

Part of the assessment of the results must come from comparison with what is already known; this information you may find in the lab manual or the course textbook, or you may have to use papers from the scientific literature. The key thing here is that you need some yardstick to judge your results. If the study is of a well-known topic, such as the effect of temperature on enzyme activity, and you are using standard materials and procedures, then differences will likely indicate problems with the work. But if the study is of something eco-logical, where your local situation may be different from the studies available for comparison, or if different species were used for experi-ments, differences are to be expected and do not necessarily indicate a problem. Either way, you must suggest what factors could have caused the differences.

Finish the Discussion section by drawing your conclusion about the hypotheses and relating it to the Introduction. Don't make grandiose claims for a modest experiment. You don't have to pretend that your experiment or observations advanced science, and it looks silly if you do. And don't conclude that what happened was that you learned how (or how not!) to do the experiment. Address the hypothesis. Your con-clusion could also include suggestions on how to improve the experi-ment, or what additional experiments would be helpful. Leave the reader with a positive message. This is the end of the text of your report, and

you want your professor to feel that the report is complete and satisfying. The worst possible way to end is just to stop at the end of a litany of errors. That way you leave the reader thinking that the lab work and the report were a mess.

Outline of Discussions of the Two Sample Papers

For the soil study, the core of the Discussion is the comparison of the two plots with each other and with any relevant literature. The topic sentences for each paragraph might be these:

⊕ Discussion
- Comparison of results from median strip and garden plot suggests that...
- Although we did not measure conditions at the two sites, there are several evident factors that could influence the abundance of soil arthropods, including extent and history of disturbance (mowing vs. tilling); fertilizer/pesticide application; presence of hydrocarbons from vehicle emissions....
- There is a known bias of Berlese funnels in extracting arthropods, among other problems with the study.
- In comparison with turf-grass fauna (Rochefort et al. 2007; ...) the median strip community...
- In comparison with tilled agricultural land (Desmond & Alex 2014; ...) the garden plots arthropod community...
- In conclusion, it is clear that differences exist in the number of arthropods in each category in the two soils. Greater differences would be expected if individuals could be identified to species and if all taxa could be identified to group....

For the endocrine study, the main features of the discussion are the effects of the herbicide and any synergistic effect, the interpretation of results for larvae versus flies, the relevance of the fruit fly results to soil arthropods, and the implication of the results to agricultural practices and soil biodiversity. In this case the topic sentences might be as follows:

⊕ Discussion
- The effect of the herbicide atrazine was as great at the highest doses as that of the insecticide carbaryl and affected especially pupation, resulting in lower numbers of pupae and flies but higher numbers of larvae....
- Larvae were more resistant than adults to carbaryl, which is a contact insecticide designed to kill adults when sprayed on them....
- Although we used standard procedures for culturing the flies, the particular strain used was chosen on the basis of its broad tolerance of environmental factors, so that results could be observed over a range of pesticide concentrations....
- We found no evidence of synergistic effects, in contrast to Thornton (2009), who studied detoxification of atrazine by *Drosophila* and subsequent susceptibility to insecticides....
- Because our studies involved mixing the pesticides with the growth media, it has clear implications for insect / arthropod communities in soil, as a great deal of sprayed pesticide enters soil as residues.
- Ideally, one would like to use actual cultures of soil organisms such as collembolids (e.g., Campiche et al. 2006) to test pesticide toxicity directly.

7 Title and Abstract

The title of the paper needs some thought, and to be sufficiently specific. For example, as a title for the pesticides experiments, "Effects of pesticides on fruit flies" is poor because it is either too vague or implies that much more was done than is the case. A more specific and effective title would be "Effects of atrazine and carbaryl on life stages of *Drosophila melanogaster*." To highlight the relevance of the study, we could add " ..., as a model for effects of endocrine disrupting chemicals on soil arthropods." Some would complain that this is too long, but long is fine provided it is concise. For the soil communities study a suitable title could be "Comparison of soil arthropod communities in two contrasting urban habitats," or " ... in highway median turf and horticultural soil." Titles often lack verbs, as you see from the examples just given, but another style is to make the title a statement of the main finding. We did that in one of our publications: "The giant zooxanthellae-bearing ciliate *Maristentor dinoferus* is closely related to Folliculinidae."

One last section you may need for your report is an abstract. Ask! The abstract is an important part of a published paper in these days of electronic retrieval because it (and the title) may be all that most readers see of the paper. Even "Notes" (short scientific papers), which often used to lack an abstract on the assumption that something short doesn't need summarizing, now usually have one for online access. Your lab report is not going to be published, and you can be sure your instructor will read it all, so perhaps it does not need an abstract. However, she may wish you to practice the skill of writing one. If so, read on.

The abstract is a self-contained synopsis of the report.

The Abstract is not a "hook" to induce the reader to keep reading, so it is unlike the first paragraph of a magazine article or English composition. Nor is it like a blurb for a book or movie, leaving the audience to anticipate the outcome. Finally, the Abstract is not the same as the "Summary" that sometimes appears at the end of a scientific paper. Such summaries cover only the conclusions.

The emphasis in an abstract is on the results and conclusions, but it also needs the centrality statement and objectives from the Introduction, and a brief summary of the Materials and Methods (unless the experiments focused on methods). It summarizes results (actual values) and conclusions; it may state the hypothesis that was supported (or refuted). Since the Abstract must be completely self-contained, it cannot include any literature citations or references to your own graphs or tables.

Abstracts are very concise, and it is an art to be able to cut as many words as possible while not sacrificing clarity. Some journals and conferences set a word limit – often 250 words. If your paper is the result of only one or two days in the lab, you should not be pressed for space.

The Abstract must be informative.

Contrast these two abstracts for a report on enzyme kinetics:

Woefully inadequate:
Michaelis-Menten plots of chymotrypsin and lysozyme activities were measured. K_m and V_{max} values were high for chymotrypsin and low for lysozyme, as expected.

Excellent:
Enzyme kinetics are widely used to study biological processes. The Michaelis constant, K_m, is a measure of the substrate concentration at which half the enzyme's activities are saturated, i.e., the efficiency of an enzyme in binding substrate. V_{max} is the maximum rate of the enzyme. In this lab, the class measured K_m and V_{max} for two enzymes with contrasting kinetics, chymotrypsin and lysozyme. Chymotrypsin is a highly active digestive enzyme, lysozyme is an antiseptic enzyme with low activity that attacks bacterial cell walls. Each enzyme and the substrates (BTEE and peptidoglycan, respectively) were commercial purified reagents. Rates were measured spectrophotometrically at a series of substrate concentrations over

the expected range of activity. The hyperbolic curves were consistent with Michaelis-Menten kinetics typical of non-regulatory enzymes. K_m values for chymotrypsin and lysozyme were 4,879 mM and 5.8 mM respectively; V_{max} values were 97 mmol s^{-1} and 0.5 mmol s^{-1} respectively, all consistent with published values. [155 words]

Following are abstracts for the two mock lab reports.

Comparison of Soil Arthropod Communities in Highway Median Turf and Horticultural Soil in [Location]

Abstract – Soil arthropod communities play key ecological roles but are readily affected by human disturbances such as tilling, fertilizing, and pesticide use. As a preliminary survey of arthropods in our local soils, we studied communities in two contrasting habitats, hypothesizing different community compositions. Soil under turfgrass in a highway median strip was subjected to regular grass removal by "weed whacker" and hydrocarbon pollution from traffic, but was not physically disturbed and apparently not subjected to fertilizers or insecticides. Soil in a community organic gardening project was regularly tilled by hand, fertilized with manure, and weeded; pesticides were never used. There was a ground cover of shredded paper. Triplicate soil samples were collected by pressing an open-ended can into the soil, and animals extracted by placing soils in Berlese funnels with a 40 W light bulb for 72 h. Specimens were sorted under dissection microscopes and identified using print and online manuals. Five major categories of arthropods could be identified but 30–35 percent remained unidentified. Mites and collembolids dominated, but there were more collembolids and fewer mites in garden soil and the opposite in the median strip. Berlese funnels are a standard method for extracting soil arthropods but may bias the results, since the conditions used may have caused some animals to die in the soil and others to be unmotivated to migrate. Use of additional methods and improved taxonomy would yield more reliable results and should be worked out before extensive surveying of local soil habitats is undertaken. [248 words]

Effects of Atrazine and Carbaryl on Life Stages of *Drosophila melanogaster* as a Model for Effects of Endocrine-Disrupting Chemicals on Soil Arthropods

Abstract – Atrazine (RoundUp®) and carbaryl (Sevin®) are widely used pesticides, atrazine used as a broadleaf weed killer in grain fields and carbaryl as a general purpose contact insecticide. Both are known endocrine-disrupting chemicals (EDCs). In order to assess the effects of the two pesticides alone and in combination, we used as a model organism the fruit fly *Drosophila melanogaster*, yellow phenotype. We hypothesized that (a) the herbicide would impact fly development and (b) there would be synergistic effects, as reported in the literature. Five female and four male flies were inoculated into standard culture vials containing nutrient medium mixed with atrazine and/or carbaryl in a dilution series of 40, 4, 0.4 and 0 ppm. Trials were run in triplicate. The numbers of larvae, pupae, and adult flies in each vial were counted weekly over 5 weeks. Pivot tables in Excel® were used to arrange the data in ways that allowed easy display of results. The herbicide was toxic at all concentrations and at 40 ppm as toxic as the insecticide in reducing the numbers of flies and pupae. The numbers of larvae showed an apparently opposite response, explained by a hypothesis that the EDCs inhibited pupation, and therefore prevented metamorphosis to adults. The results suggest that fruit flies are an appropriate model for testing EDC effects on arthropods, but ideally one would use cultured soil arthropods, such as collembolids. [230 words]

PART III

Crafting the Final Version
Scientific Style

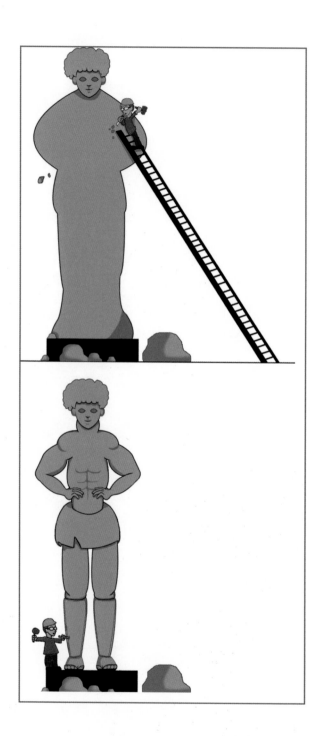

8 Revising Your Paper

Looking Back Over the Whole First Draft

If you have worked through Part II, you now have a complete text for your report. It is in the proper format but the style may be rough. Set this draft aside for a day or two, if possible, so that you can come back to it with a critical eye. (If you cannot wait that long, at least do something else for a few hours – exercise, meditate, or relax!)

Improving the Content

First, read through the report to get the big picture. Consciously think about large aspects. For a start, does it have all its parts in the right order? Flip through and check them off:

Title and your name
Abstract (if needed)
Introduction (with objectives)
Materials and Methods
Results (only your results)
Discussion (with a conclusion)
Acknowledgments (if needed)
References
Tables (numbered and with titles at the top and any necessary
    notes at the bottom)
Figures (numbered and with captions underneath or on a
    separate page)

Next, go over the structure carefully:

Is each section complete? If you were shifting back and forth between sections or were hurrying, you may have left out something. Try not to overlook the obvious.

Is all the expected content present? Follow the hypotheses from Introduction, through Materials and Methods, Results, and Discussion to see that the story is complete.

Do the sequences of ideas in the Introduction and Discussion flow, with smooth transitions between them (see Fig. 3.1)? Ask yourself at the start of each paragraph, "Does this follow from the last paragraph?" And, "Is everything in this paragraph about the topic?" Make sure that each paragraph starts with a clear topic sentence that is then elaborated with relevant details.

Have you given enough background in the Introduction so that the rationale for the objectives is clear?

Does the Discussion evaluate the results and state the conclusion about the hypotheses you tested?

Are the graphs and tables complete and properly designed? Is each cited in order? Did you avoid duplication? Could you reduce any to a sentence?

Results versus Discussion

Although some journals allow combined Results and Discussion, most demand separate sections, and your professor likely did, too. Ask! The Results section should include only what you found. The Discussion includes what the results mean. However, the distinction between the results themselves and their interpretation is not always sharp. Sometimes the way you write a sentence will convert a result into a conclusion. Consider why the following phrasing is a conclusion, not a result: "Temperature had no effect on respiration." What you observed was that, "Respiration rate was $a \pm b$ at all temperatures tested." The conclusion includes an assumption that no other factor masked any effect of temperature.

Statements of values will usually give only results; statements that involve comments on cause and effect are probably conclusions. Another clue to Discussion elements in the Results is any reference to the literature. The Results should contain only your data.

While the difference between Results and Discussion may seem a small point in writing, it bears on an important scientific issue. We don't always distinguish between observations and conclusions in everyday life – we often see only part of an event and fill in the rest. We could not operate if our brains did not function this way. Our safety and survival may depend on quick assumptions (this is why police use racial profiling and have the unfortunate maxim to "shoot first and ask questions later"). However, as scientists (and even in everyday life), we need to be able to recognize the difference between observations and conclusions (see Box 8.1)

8.1 Sherlock Holmes, the Master of Inferences

"Doctor Watson, Mr. Sherlock Holmes," said Stamford, introducing us.

"How are you?" he said cordially, gripping my hand. "You have been in Afghanistan, I perceive."

"How on earth did you know that?" I asked in astonishment.

"Observation with me is second nature," he observed. "From long habit the train of thoughts ran so swiftly through my mind that I arrived at the conclusion without being conscious of intermediate steps. There were such steps, however. The train of reasoning ran, 'Here is a gentleman of the medical type, but with the air of a military man. Clearly an army doctor, then. He has just come from the tropics, for his face is dark, and that is not the natural tint of his skin, for his wrists are fair. He has undergone hardship and sickness, as his haggard face says clearly. His left arm has been injured. He holds it in a stiff and unnatural manner. Where in the tropics [in 1880] could an English army doctor have seen much hardship and got his arm wounded? Clearly in Afghanistan.'"

"It is simple enough as you explain it," I exclaimed.

"I am an expert at drawing inferences," he declared.

Adapted from "A Study in Scarlet" by Arthur Conan Doyle.
A twenty-first-century version of this conversation is included in the BBC TV
Sherlock episode, "Study in Pink."

Improving the Style: Straightforward and Clear

Whenever you read through your paper you should be alert for grammatical and spelling errors. In addition, you should read through the paper once to consider the writing carefully and to give it a final polish.

A GAZELLE CAN JUMP HIGHER THAN THE AVERAGE HOUSE *

*This is because the average house cannot jump.

Ambiguities can be funny, but in scientific writing clarity is valued over humor.

However, the main thing is to present your scientific work clearly. You need not belabor style, particularly composition style, by trying to think of more elegant ways to express yourself. Check spelling and basic grammar, and allow your sense of style to develop gradually.

Five points of scientific style need special mention. These are: conciseness, tense, the use of the passive voice, tentative language, and terms from Latin and Greek.

1 Scientific Writing is Concise

Concise means expressing much briefly – it is not simply short. Never sacrifice clarity for the sake of brevity. If the sentence becomes so condensed that the reader has to fill in words to make sense of it, there is a great risk of ambiguity. This is why headlines or classified ads are sometimes funny. Look for dangling participles, dangling pronouns, ambiguous antecedents, and missing punctuation. Eliminate repetition and wordiness and check that every sentence is unambiguous.

2 The Question of Tense

In the Introduction you will sometimes be writing about things that have been established or are accepted by the scientific community; such statements should be in the present tense, as in the two sample centrality statements in Chapter 3. At other times you will be writing about what people did or found. For example, "Barberena-Arias et al. (2012) **studied** the effectiveness of different methods of collecting soil arthropods" or "The herbicide diuron **was found** to be toxic to *Folsomia candida* (Campiche et al. 2006)."

Materials and Methods (Chapter 4) and Results (Chapter 5) are written almost entirely in past tense, because these sections describe what you did and what you found (one exception would be where you are describing characteristics of the organism used).

3 Active or Passive Voice?

The passive voice makes the object of the action the subject of the sentence: "Five bottles were filled." The real subject, assumed to be you, as author of the report, is omitted. Science papers are often written in the passive voice. However, there are divergent and often strong opinions about whether use of the passive is good or bad. Ask what your professor wants! One of our colleagues aggressively promotes the passive. ("The report is about the experiment, not about you!" she exclaims.) Another colleague equally hotly denounces use of the passive as "Victorian prudery" that leads to "committee writing [style], ponderous discussions, and avoidance of responsibility." The passive can be cumbersome, wordy, and dull unless skillfully written; passive sentences may be confusing or even pompous. Nevertheless, the standard for scientific writing is to use passive voice and avoid personal pronouns, so you should practice using it. Use active verbs when appropriate, and your sentences will be clearer and more direct. The examples for the model lab reports and the published papers analyzed in Chapter 10 generally use the passive; analyze the three abstracts in Chapter 7 to see which sentences have passive verbs and which have active verbs. For example, active [A] and passive [P] verbs are flagged in this excerpt:

> Soil arthropod communities **play** [A] key ecological roles but **are** readily **affected** [P] by human disturbances such as tilling, fertilizing, and pesticide use. As a preliminary survey of arthropods in our local soils, **we studied** [A] communities in two contrasting habitats, hypothesizing different community compositions. Soil under turfgrass in a highway median strip **was subjected** [P] to regular grass removal by "weed whacker" and hydrocarbon pollution from traffic, but **was** not physically **disturbed** [P] and apparently not **subjected** [P] to fertilizers or insecticides.

4 Tentative Language

As we explained in Chapter 1, there is always some level of uncertainty, especially in conclusions. Thus appropriate words or phrases must be used to qualify the claims. Biologists do not speak of proving things. You may *show* that under specified conditions respiration in a sample of species X had a particular response to temperature. But your results are interesting only inasmuch as they tell us about how *any* sample of species X will behave, or even more interesting, what this tells us about the response of other, similar organisms. Science is interested in general principles, not specific things that happened once in your lab. The further you extend your conclusions, the more tentative they become. See Chapter 1 for examples of tentative language.

5 Latin and Greek Words, and Words from Those Languages

Check singulars and plurals, especially of words with Latin or Greek origins: Data are plural (unless you have only one datum point, in which case you have a bigger problem than grammar). So are media (singular = medium), mitochondria (mitochondrion), criteria (criterion), and flagella (flagellum). But not all Latin-looking words ending in –a are plural! Examples include alga (plural = algae), seta (setae), stoma (stomata), and stigma (stigmata), among others; the last two of these are from Greek, hence the –ata plural ending.

Species binomials are Latin (or Latinized) and are always written in italics, with the genus name capitalized and the species not, as in *Homo sapiens*.

Citations

There are several methods for citing literature, and you must follow one method consistently. The commonest and easiest is the author–date format: Love (1996). Ask! Some journals save space by using the numbered method, numbering references either consecutively through the text or according to the alphabetical listing in the References. Whatever method you use (your professor may have specified; if not we suggest you use author–date), you must keep the sentence flow smooth. Citations, especially several author–date citations in a row, tend to break up the text. Put them at the ends of sentences, or at least at the ends of clauses. Don't break up clauses unless you absolutely must.

You can either use the author's name as part of the sentence – "Love (1996) listed four types of ... " or, usually more concisely, put both name and date in parentheses – "There are 4 types of explanation in science textbooks (Love 1996)." If you have more than one paper by the same author(s) in one year, distinguish them by "a" and "b" (Author 1999a). Do not include the author's initials in the citation unless you need to distinguish two first authors with the same last name (e.g., K. Smith 1999 from N. Smith 1999).

For two authors, you can use "and" or "&" between them. For a lab report the choice is trivial; just be consistent. Also be consistent about whether or not you put a comma before the date: (Love, 1996) or (Love 1996). If a paper has three or more authors, abbreviate using et al. (short for *et alii*, which means "and others"): Palacios-Vargas et al. (2007). In most journals, et al. is not printed in italics (likewise for many other abbreviations taken from Latin, e.g., i.e., c.v., etc.).

You should not give the page number in citations, even for a book (i.e., not Love 1996: 159), in contrast to practice in other disciplines. The one exception is when you use a direct quotation. However, it is a good idea to note the page for your own reference when you make notes from a source, so that you can easily return to the exact location.

Grammar and Syntax

Think in PARAGRAPHS and create TOPIC SENTENCES.

If you have been using outlines, you may already have a good set of topic sentences. It should be possible to read the first sentence of each paragraph and understand the progress of the discourse. Ask yourself, what is this paragraph about? Make a clear statement to express that. Then gather all the sentences relating to that topic, excluding all others. Organize them with clear connections, keeping in mind Gopen and Swan's (1990) insight into topic and stress parts of each sentence (Chapter 3). Do not write single-sentence paragraphs. Do not mix themes within one paragraph.

There are many guides to proper usage of English, including some for science writers. This is not the place for us to teach you academic English, but below we highlight a few key points drawn from Woodford (1968) and Gastel and Day (2016).

The Council of Biology Editors' book *Scientific Writing for Graduate Students* (Woodford 1968; still the standard) gives rules, with exercises on each, for polishing style. We have excerpted the following three, with permission:

Make sure of the meaning of every word, especially pairs like varying/ various; affect/effect. There are lists in the *CBE Style Manual* and in

Gastel and Day (2016). The context of the word may be as important as the meaning of the word itself. For instance:

> The tubes were shaken, followed by centrifugation, and the upper phase withdrawn.

(Were the tubes followed by centrifugation? Was the upper phase withdrawn?)

Use verbs instead of abstract nouns. For example, separate rather than separation. Releasing the hidden verb makes the sentence shorter and more vigorous:

> Primary and secondary particle separation was obtained by electrophoresis.

becomes:

> Primary and secondary particles were separated by electrophoresis.

Break up noun clusters and stacked modifiers. Your sentence may be longer, but it will be clearer. The longer the string, the less intelligible it becomes. For instance:

> Highly purified heavy beef heart mitochondria protein ...

is too concise – what modifies what? In this case the meaning is:

> Protein from the highly purified heavy fraction of bovine heart mitochondria ...

Gastel and Day (2016) give Ten Commandments of good writing, humorously incorporating the fault into the commandment:

1. Each pronoun should agree with their antecedent.
2. Just between you and i, case is important.
3. A preposition is a poor word to end a sentence with.
4. Verbs has to agree with their subject.
5. Don't use no double negatives.
6. Remember to never split an infinitive.
7. When dangling, don't use participles.
8. Join clauses good, like a conjunction should.
9. Don't write a run-on sentence it is difficult when you got to punctuate it so it makes sense when the reader reads what you wrote.
10. About sentence fragments.

9 References

Scientists who write papers for publication have learned to deal with the exacting details of citation and references style demanded by journals. Your professor may wish you to begin learning the style now. He or she may be more concerned, however, that you use the literature and write a good report than that you write out references in some precise format. Ask! Correct information is more important than correct arrangement of the items.

Check the Information Carefully!

The first step in finishing the reference list is to check through your report and make sure all works that you cited are listed. Do not create a bibliography – that is, a list of pertinent works which you consulted but did not cite.

Make sure you copy the references correctly, especially the volume number and page numbers. As you use books and papers to track down others you will quickly learn that a mistake in a reference can be extremely frustrating and time-wasting.

The list of references follows the Discussion (and Acknowledgments, if any). In the author–date format, the references must be arranged in alphabetical order of the names of the first authors (who are also sometimes called the "senior" authors, regardless of their relative ages!).

Indent the second and subsequent lines of each reference (see samples below). This is called a hanging indent; do not format with tabs and line breaks! Do not start a new line for the date or title (in contrast to styles common in the humanities).

JOURNAL ARTICLE (assume the journal title is to be given in full)
Palacios-Vargas, J.G., Castaño-Meneses, G., Gómez-Anaya, J.A., Martínez-Yrizar, A., Mejía-Recamia, B.E., & Martínez-Sanchez, J. 2007. Litter and soil arthropods diversity and density in a tropical dry forest ecosystem in Western Mexico. *Biodiversity and Conservation* 16: 3703–3717.

WEB PAGE (note that the date you view the web page is included because URLs change)
Moldenke A.R. n.d. Soil arthropods. www.nrcs.usda.gov/wps/portal/nrcs/detailfull/soils/health/biology/?cid=nrcs142p2_053861, accessed 4 January 2016.
If you find an electronic copy of a print article on the internet, cite the print source rather than the URL.

BOOK
Lobban, C.S., Schefter, M., Camacho, F.A., & Jocson, J. 2014. *Tropical Pacific Island Environments,* 2nd ed. Bess Press, Honolulu, HI, USA.

CHAPTER IN A BOOK
Love, A. 1996. How do we explain explanation? An examination of the concept of "explanation" in relation to the communication needs of science undergraduates. In, Hewings, M. & Dudley-Evans, T. (eds.), *Evaluation and Course Design in EAP.* Prentice Hall-Macmillan in association with the British Council, Hemel Hempstead, UK, pp. 151–165.

Order for References

In addition to alphabetizing by first author, use the following rules for arranging the references:

More than one paper by the same author:
put in chronological order
More than one paper in the same year by the same author:
number a, b (the order doesn't matter, just be sure the letters correspond to the citations in the text)
Dual author names with same first author:
alphabetize according to the second author

More than one paper by author et al., even if the coauthors are
    different:
    put in chronological order regardless of et al.'s names
More than one author with the same last name:
    alphabetize according to author initials

The following sample list is correctly arranged according to these rules:

Adams, K. 2008.
Adams, K. 2010a.
Adams, K. 2010b.
Adams, N. 1995.
Adams, N. & Smyth, B. 2009.
Adams, N. & Wong, K. 2006.
Adams, N., Brown, L. & Smyth, B. 2013. [Adams et al. 2013]
Adams, N., Adams, K. & Adams, Z. 2015. [Adams et al. 2015]

Reference Lists for the Two Mock Lab Reports

PESTICIDES STUDY
References

Campiche, S., Becker-van Slooten, K., Ridreau, C. & Tarradellas, J. 2006. Effects of insect growth regulators on the nontarget soil arthropod *Folsomia candida* (Collembola). *Ecotoxicology and Environmental Safety* 63: 216–225.

Jennings, B.H. 2011. *Drosophila:* A versatile model in biology and medicine. *Materials Today* 14: 190–195.

Menta, C. 2012. Soil fauna diversity: Function, soil degradation, biological indices, soil restoration. In: Lameed, G.A. (ed.), *Biodiversity Conservation and Utilization in a Diverse World.* InTech Online Publisher, www.intechopen.com, pp. 59–94.

Mnif, W., Hassine, A.I.H., Bouaziz, A., Bartegi, A., Thomas, O., & Roig, B. 2011. Effect of endocrine disruptor pesticides: A review. *International Journal of Environmental Research and Public Health* 8: 2265–2303.

Thornton, B.J. 2009. Sex-dependent changes in activity of detoxification enzymes, insecticide susceptibility, and alterations in protein expression induced by atrazine in *Drosophila melanogaster.* Dissertation, University of Nebraska. www.southern.edu/biology/Documents/Thornton/Dissertation.Thornton.pdf, accessed 10 May 2016.

SOIL ARTHROPODS STUDY

References

Ashford, O.S., Foster, W.A., Turner, B.L., Sayer, E.J., Sutcliffe, L., & Tanner, E.V.J. 2013. Litter manipulation and the soil arthropod community in a lowland tropical rainforest. *Soil Biology and Biochemistry* 62: 5–12

Barberena-Arias, M.F., González, G., & Cuevas, E. 2012. Quantifying variation of soil arthropods using different sampling protocols: Is diversity affected? In Sudarshana, P., Nageswara-Rao, M., & Soneji, J.R. (eds.), *Tropical Forest*. InTech Online Publisher, www .intechopen.com, pp. 51–70.

Desmond, A.O. & Alex, U.O. 2013. Comparative assessment of soil arthropod abundance and diversity in practical farmlands of University of Ibadan, Nigeria. *International Journal of Environmental Resources Research* 1: 17–29.

Longino, J.T. & Colwell, R.K. 1997. Biodiversity assessment using structured inventory: Capturing the ant fauna of a tropical rain forest. *Ecological Applications* 7: 1263–1277.

Menta, C. 2012. Soil fauna diversity: Function, soil degradation, biological indices, soil restoration. In Lameed, G.A. (ed.), *Biodiversity Conservation and Utilization in a Diverse World*. InTech Online Publisher, www.intechopen.com, pp. 59–94.

Rochefort, S., Therrien, F., Shetlar, D.J., & Brodeur, J. 2006. Species diversity and seasonal abundance of Collembola in turfgrass ecosystems in North America. *Pedobiologia* 50: 61–68.

When you have polished the text of your report to your satisfaction, and completed the references, you are ready to "package" it:

1. double-space everything, including references and tables;
2. proofread one last time for typographical errors ...

... and hand it in. **Congratulations!**

PART IV

The Anatomy of Scientific Papers

10 Transitioning to Writing about Original Research

Soon in your scientific apprenticeship you will have opportunities to conduct original research, where the outcome is unknown even to the professor. There are many books that go into great detail on how to prepare a report on such work for publication, and that is beyond the scope of our book. The differences from what you learned here are not great, since you have already been testing hypotheses and using the scientific format for your reports. There is, however, a great deal to learn to craft a professional-caliber manuscript, and that is an art that you will practice many times in your career. Even scientists who have published scores of papers continue to learn from the peer-review process and we all expect to get useful comments from the reviewers and editors about better expressing our ideas.

There is a scientific rationale for an original research study.

The first major difference is in the Introduction. First, how the "centrality statement" is written depends on the journal to which you plan to submit the paper. For example, in the two papers on soil arthropods analyzed below, the one that was submitted to a journal of soil science did not need to point out the importance of arthropods to the ecology and well-being of soil, unlike the one published in a journal covering the broad spectrum of biodiversity conservation, where readers might not know about soil arthropods. Second, the selection of relevant literature differs. It still needs to both introduce the subject (and sometimes the methods) to the reader and to show that the authors know what has been done before of relevance, but a few general references will not suffice. Editors and reviewers of submitted manuscripts will expect you to be up to date on the literature, and since the reviewers are chosen because they are experts in the particular subject matter, they will know the literature (and have contributed to it)! So when you write the background information in the Introduction you should make every effort to include all the relevant works, at least representative papers (e.g., reviews) by those who have worked in the field, while still being concise. You should have read those works as you prepared for and worked through your study, because these are the studies you are building on, and because you need to establish that your study has not been done before. The literature review then concludes with a "gap analysis" – that is, having described what is known about your topic, you then state what is not known. Typically, this gap is bigger than your study can fill by itself, but it shows how you are contributing to advancing understanding of the subject.

A second major difference is in the Materials and Methods, again because of the different readership. In the lab reports you have written so far, the reader was your instructor, who set up the lab work, and your report had to show that you understood and followed the procedures given to you. In a professional report of original research, it is assumed that the readers already have a professional level of knowledge about general methods, but they don't know what you did and they might want to try your methods in their own research. Thus, the important details are what instruments were used, such as what brand and model spectrophotometer, since that might make a difference to the accuracy or reliability of the results; but one would not mention the details of how a 1.5 M solution was prepared unless there was some unusual difficulty.

The Results section is more complicated because you will probably have a lot more data (perhaps not all of it relevant to a particular report), which need to be summarized and interpreted before you can state what the results were and select appropriate graphs and tables to present as supporting evidence.

Finally, the Discussion must include detailed comparison with results from similar studies already published and explain the differences. Since the report establishes new findings, the authors are expected to extend their conclusions as far as is reasonable, using appropriate tentative language.

It is also common to find an Acknowledgments section in which funding agencies are credited and any people or agencies who provided special help but did not have sufficient input to warrant co-authorship are thanked.

Given that there are two broad kinds of study – experimental and observational (Chapter 1) – we present below excerpts from one publication of each kind, annotated to show the major structural features. They are intended primarily to show you the format of a published report. As you develop your science writing skills, you can also study the writing style. Even though you may not understand some words and concepts, you should be able to follow the main ideas using our annotations.

Anatomy of an Observational Paper

Citation for this paper is:

Palacios-Vargas, J.G., Castaño-Meneses, G., Gómez-Anaya, J.A., Martínez-Yrízar, A., Mejía-Recamia, B.E., & Martínez-Sanchez, J. 2007. Litter and soil arthropods diversity and density in a tropical dry forest ecosystem in Western Mexico. *Biodiversity and Conservation* 16: 3703–3717.

In this paper, the authors studied the kinds and quantities of arthropods living in the leaf litter and soil in two watersheds in the tropical dry forest of Western Mexico. They looked for correlations between seasonal abundances and rainfall and temperature, and they compared their results with those from both tropical rainforests and temperate forests.

Biodivers Conserv (2007) 16:3703–3717
DOI 10.1007/s10531-006-9109-7

ORIGINAL PAPER

Litter and soil arthropods diversity and density in a tropical dry forest ecosystem in Western Mexico

J. G. Palacios-Vargas · G. Castaño-Meneses ·
J. A. Gómez-Anaya · A. Martínez-Yrizar ·
B. E. Mejía-Recamier · J. Martínez-Sánchez

Received: 19 April 2005 / Accepted: 25 May 2006 / Published online: 10 August 2007
© Springer Science+Business Media B.V. 2007

Abstract The composition and temporal changes of edaphic microarthropods in both litter layer and soil were analyzed in a tropical dry forest ecosystem in Western Mexico. Sampling was carried out from June 1991 to July 1992 in two small watersheds at the Chamela Biological Station (Jalisco State, Mexico). At each watershed 10 random cores samples, 11 cm in diameter and 5 cm depth, were taken monthly from each biotope from an area of 100 m^2. Fauna was extracted by Berlese-Tullgren funnels and preserved in 75% ethanol. The total abundance of arthropods was 96,338 specimens, belonging to 33 taxa. Numerically dominant groups were Prostigmata, Cryptostigmata, Collembola and Mesostigmata, which constituted 92.6% of the total abundance. The effect of current monthly precipitation and temperature on density of total Arthropoda and different Orders was also investigated. Precipitation and temperature were significantly correlated with Collembola and Mesostigmata densities and also with total arthropod. The seasonal variation in the amount of litterfall was also significantly related to the abundance of arthropod in the litter layer biotope.

Note that the Introduction has the following structure:

- The first paragraph is the centrality statement.
- Paragraphs 2–4 (3 omitted) provide the general background, dealing with conclusions that apply generally, and ending with statements about North America and wet tropical forests that can be compared/ contrasted with their area.
- Paragraph 4 turns attention to the forests under study, and then expresses a need for data; the last sentence is the gap analysis.
- The final paragraph states the objectives of the study. The hypotheses are not directly stated, but would be understood by the reader. For example, H_1: the arthropod diversity and density are similar to those in temperate forests; H_0: the arthropod diversity and density

differ from those in temperate forests. And, H_1: arthropod density is related to current precipitation; H_0: arthropod density is not related to current precipitation.

Notice the use of tense in the first paragraph of the Introduction: the first sentence states some well-established conclusions about the real world and is in the present tense; the second, because the conclusions are only about artificial microcosms, is in the past tense. Notice how tense is used in the rest of the Introduction.

Introduction

Microarthropods living in the litter layer and in the upper strata of the soil are an important component of the ecosystem, because of their relevant role as regulators of key functional processes, such as organic matter decomposition and mineralization (Whitford and Parker 1989; Kaczmarek et al. 1995), nutrient cycling (Irmler 1982) and soil formation (Persson 1989). Soil fauna has also been shown in microcosms to affect plant species diversity as a result of selective feeding on roots and mycorrhizal fungi (De Deyn et al. 2003).

Soil fauna diversity and abundance has been used as an indication of soil stress; many edaphic microarthropods taxa can be used as bioindicators of soil health or quality (Iglisch 1981; Van Straalen and Verhoef 1997; Parisi et al. 2005). Thus, recent research has examined in experimental plots the possible effects of global change on soil fauna abundance and diversity and the consequences of land use change and soil disturbance (Lindberg et al. 2002; Petersen et al. 2004).

Tropical dry forest ecosystems comprise more than 40% of tropical forest areas of the world (Murphy and Lugo 1986). Unfortunately, there has been a rapid increase of loss of forest area in recent years as a result of accelerated anthropogenic disturbance (Janzen 1988; Trejo and Dirzo 2000). The average rate of soil erosion in the tropical dry forest along the Mexican Pacific Coast is very high, and in particular, for the Chamela Biological Station, rates vary from 0.19 ± 0.15 Mg ha^{-1} y^{-1} to 13.2 ± 0.8 Mg ha^{-1} y^{-1} (Maass et al. 1988; García-Oliva et al. 1995). Therefore, in order to determine the ecological significance of the soil fauna in the tropical dry forest ecosystem in this region, there is an urgent need to document not only its taxonomic composition (Palacios-Vargas and Mejía 1988; PalaciosVargas and Díaz 1995), but also its population density, seasonality and patterns of activity, aspects that have received only very limited attention of study (Pescador-Rubio et al. 2002).

The main objective of this study is to identify and compare the composition, density and seasonal changes of soil and litter arthropods in two tropical dry forest watersheds located in the Tropical Biological Station of Chamela, in the Pacific coast of Jalisco, Mexico. The relationship between Arthropod density and current precipitation, temperature, forest litterfall and standing crop litter was also investigated.

The Materials and Methods section is presented in several sections, dealing in turn with a description of the study area, the procedures for data collection, and the statistical analyses.

Materials and methods

Study area

The Chamela Biological Station (ChBS) of the Instituto de Biología of Universidad Nacional Autónoma de México (UNAM) is a nature reserve located on the coast of the state of Jalisco, México (19°30′ N, 105°03′ W; 150 m elevation). The rainy season comprises 4 months, mainly from July to October (Bullock 1986). Mean annual precipitation and temperature are 788 mm and 24.6°C, respectively (1977–2000; García-

Data collection

Sampling was carried out in both litter layer and soil, from June 1991 to July 1992 in Watershed 1 and Watershed 4, two of five contiguous small watersheds (12–28 ha) gauged for long-term ecosystem research (Cervantes et al. 1988). We used a circular sampler (11 cm in diameter and 5 cm in depth), to collect monthly 10 soil cores from each watershed in each biotope that made a total of 480 samples. Leaf litter fraction on the top of each core was collected first and then the corresponding vertical soil portion. Sampling points were selected randomly within a 100 m^2 area on the middle portion of each

Data analysis

Overall fauna community structure was based on percentage of abundance. After being tested for normality and homogeneity of variances, taxa density was compared with a threeway ANOVA model. A Tukey's test was used to compare watersheds, biotopes and months (Manly 1998).

ANOVA test was used to evaluate watershed differences in mean annual litterfall and

---

Similarly, the Results section is divided with several subheadings, dealing in turn with forest litter, (overall) fauna abundance, (details of) Arthropoda, excluding Collembola and Acari, and then Collembola and Acari, the two most abundant groups.

Here is a sample of the Results, the section on Collembola, along with part of the table referred to and the figure.

Collembola

A total of 24,253 springtails were collected in both biotopes (Table 1). Twelve families were recorded from which Isotomidae (29.3%) and Entomobryidae (28.9%) out-numbered all others. There was not a significant difference in Collembola density between biotopes ($F = 1.24$; df = 1,456; $P > 0.05$). However, there was a significant difference among the collecting months ($F = 22.67$; df = 11,446; $P < 0.001$), mainly due to the high Collembola density recorded in January (Fig. 5).

Collembola density in the soil biotope was significantly correlated with temperature ($r = -0.34$; df = 227; $P < 0.01$), and with precipitation and temperature in the litter biotope ($r = 0.59$; df = 227; $P < 0.01$), ($r = -0.31$; df = 227; $P < 0.01$), respectively. Collembola density was also correlated with the amount of litterfall ($r = 0.35$; df = 208; $P < 0.005$).

Taxa	Abundance (number of specimens)		Density ind m^{-2}		Percentage	
	S	L	S	L	S	L
Prostigmata	19,392	10,215	8,505	4,480	32.10	28.43
Cryptostigmata	18,896	9,748	8,289	4,275	31.28	27.13
Collembola	13,330	10,923	5,846	4,791	22.06	30.40
Mesostigmata	4,325	1,613	1,897	707	7.16	4.50
Total	60,413	35,925	26,497	15,756	100	100
H′			1.64	1.68		
J′			0.49	0.48		
S			28	32		

H′ = Shannon's diversity index, J′ = Pielou's evenness index, S = Species richness

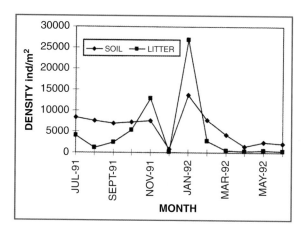

The Discussion starts out with the main conclusion:

Discussion

Arthropoda communities in the litter layer and soil biotope at the Chamela forest were dominated by Acari (mainly Prostigmata and Cryptostigmata) and Collembola. These groups of microarthropods are known to be important in the trophic interactions of the soil biota affecting the availability of soil nutrients for plant growth (Persson 1989). They are also important in the process of plant litter decomposition and soil microstructure formation (Rusek 1998; Lussenhop and BassiriRad 2005).

It then compares the main findings with results from temperate forests and rainforests as reported in the literature. Notice that their findings corroborate the tropical–temperate pattern, but the densities were different.

Based on the general patterns of composition and abundance of the soil fauna invertebrates found in different ecosystems, it has been suggested that compared to the macrofauna (body size > 1 cm length) which is more abundant in tropical ecosystems, the microfauna (<1 cm) is the predominant group in temperate ecosystems (González and Seastedt 2000). Although microarthropods in Chamela are the more abundant groups as in temperate ecosystems, the densities are lower in Chamela than reported in temperate forests. Kübelböck (1982) found similar results in dominant groups from soils of Venezuela as recorded in Chamela, and O'Lear and Blair (1999) from tallgrass prairie soils in Kansas. Dominant groups (prostigmatid and oribatid mites) in the Chamela biotopes constituted up to 65% of total microarthropods. Collembola was the third dominant group and along with all the Orders of mites, they made up 90% of total microarthropods. In contrast to Chamela, in the seasonal lowland coastal forests of eastern Tanzania, over 50% of the leaf litter fauna are Collembola and Acari (Burgess et al. 1999).

Later, they interpret the findings and comment on their confidence in the conclusion.

> Overall, our density Arthropoda values are higher than those recorded in a humid tropical forest, but lower than those found in temperate ecosystems (Haarlow 1960; Lebrun 1971). Therefore, it is possible that the tropical dry forest ecosystem could be considered an intermediate condition regarding soil arthropods total density. However, the level of confidence for this assertion remains limited by the small number of studies with complete estimates of soil arthropods density and composition in forest ecosystems.

The Discussion ends with a concluding paragraph, and the paper then ends with Acknowledgments and References.

> Our results constitute an important base to understand the dynamics of the soil microarthropod community in the seasonal tropical forest, which can help conservation plans in an area with severe deforestation problems.

Anatomy of an Experimental Paper

Citation for this paper is:

Campiche, S., Becker-van Slooten, K., Ridreau, C., & Tarradellas, J. 2006. Effects of insect growth regulators on the nontarget soil arthropod *Folsomia candida* (Collembola). *Ecotoxicology and Environmental Safety* 63: 216–225.

In this paper, the authors studied the impact of several insecticides on a representative collembolid. Collembolids are hexapod Arthropoda, but in a different class from Insecta, thus are closely related to insects but by definition are not targets of insecticides. In most soils, as in the Mexican dry forest studied in the sample observational paper on the preceding pages, collembolids are one of the two groups of arthropods that dominate soil communities. The other big group is the Acari, or mites – these are insects. In practice, soil mites are also nontarget, since insecticides are designed to target agricultural pest insects, but being insects, they will be affected when the pesticides drip down into the soil.

ELSEVIER

Available online at www.sciencedirect.com

SCIENCE @ DIRECT®

Ecotoxicology and Environmental Safety 63 (2006) 216–225

Ecotoxicology
and
Environmental
Safety

www.elsevier.com/locate/ecoenv

Effects of insect growth regulators on the nontarget soil arthropod *Folsomia candida* (Collembola)

S. Campiche*, K. Becker-van Slooten, C. Rideau, J. Tarradellas

Ecole Polytechnique Fédérale de Lausanne, ENAC-ISTE, Laboratory of Environmental Chemistry and Ecotoxicology, Station 2, CH-1015 Lausanne, Switzerland

Received 18 January 2005; received in revised form 19 May 2005; accepted 6 July 2005

Abstract

The aim of this study was to assess the effect of several insect growth regulators (IGRs) on the nontarget soil arthropod *Folsomia candida* (Collembola). The survival and reproduction rates of *F. candida* were evaluated after 28 days of exposure to six IGRs (methoprene, fenoxycarb, precocene II, tebufenozide, hexaflumuron and teflubenzuron) and to one herbicide (diuron) in artificial soil. The differences in the sensitivity of *F. candida* to these different substances are high. The chitin synthesis inhibitors teflubenzuron and hexaflumuron were the most toxic compounds with an EC50 of 0.05 mg/kg (dry weight) for teflubenzuron and an EC50 of 0.6 mg/kg for hexaflumuron. Teflubenzuron is toxic for *F. candida* at concentrations that are probably close to environmental levels of this insecticide. Inhibition of reproduction is strongly related to adult survival for the juvenile hormone agonist methoprene and for the antijuvenile hormone precocene II, with an EC50 of 173 mg/kg and a LC50 of 178 mg/kg for methoprene and an EC50 of 15 mg/kg and a LC50 of 26 mg/kg for precocene II. Fenoxycarb, another juvenile hormone analog, showed a dose–response curve for mortality different from that of methoprene; at concentrations such as 3052 mg/kg no effect on adult survival was observed. However, the EC50 value of 113 mg/kg is of the same order of magnitude as that obtained for methoprene. A test with compressed soil contaminated with fenoxycarb was conducted to observe parameters such as numbers of eggs laid and juveniles hatched. No differences were observed between these two endpoints for fenoxycarb. An EC50 of 109 mg/kg was obtained for the ecdysone agonist tebufenozide. The herbicide diuron showed a relatively high toxicity for *F. candida* with an EC50 of 20 mg/kg. Our results show that some of the tested IGRs can have effects on Collembola at environmentally relevant concentrations (toxicity/exposure ratios <5 for teflubenzuron, hexaflumuron, and diuron).

The Introduction has the following structure:

- The first paragraph is the centrality statement; notice that here the link is to pest management that is supposedly safer for food and the environment. Notice that the paragraph starts by defining the key term "insect growth regulators" (IGRs), used in the title – good use of topic and stress positions in the sentence structure (see Chapters 3 and 8; Gopen & Swan 1990).

- The second paragraph (illustrated by a figure showing the chemical structures and a table of pesticide properties) introduces the compounds involved.

- Paragraph 3 introduces the concept of endocrine-disrupting compounds (EDCs) (a broader term than IGRs), which are a major concern for the health of humans and aquatic invertebrates, and begins to define the gap in knowledge ("but hardly any information ... on soil invertebrates").

- Paragraph 4 (omitted here) gave more details on the gap and introduced some standards for testing pesticides.
- The final paragraph establishes the objectives of the study, which encompass tests of several pesticides (including one herbicide). The hypotheses are not directly stated, but would be understood by the reader. For example, H_1: fenoxycarb affects the number of eggs laid and/or juveniles hatched; H_0: fenoxycarb does not affect the number of eggs laid and/or juveniles hatched.

---

1. Introduction

Insect growth regulators (IGRs) are third-generation insecticides less toxic and compatible with insect pest management that were developed to reduce the pollution of food and environment. These compounds have a specific mode of action on insects and a lower toxicity against vertebrates than conventional insecticides (Grenier and Grenier, 1993). For this purpose, the endocrine system of insects has been intentionally targeted for insecticidal activity. The developed insecticides are used to suppress insect populations, stopping their proliferation by disrupting their normal endocrine functions (EDSTAC, 1998).

Juvenile hormone mimics (e.g., methoprene, fenoxycarb), antijuvenile hormones (e.g., precocene II), and ecdysone analogs (e.g., tebufenozide) are some examples (Fig. 1). Other IGR compounds such as teflubenzuron and hexaflumuron act preferentially by interfering with the chitin synthesis metabolism (chitin synthesis inhibitors). These substances appear to have a high target pest specificity and their effects can differ significantly among insect species (Dhadialla et al., 1998; Grenier and Grenier, 1993). Some IGRs are considered highly toxic ($LC50$ $100-1000$ $\mu g/L$ for tebufenozide) to very highly toxic ($LC50 < 100$ $\mu g/L$ for fenoxycarb and methoprene) for aquatic insects (http://docs.pesticideinfo.org/Index.html, 2004). Their other major characteristics are summarized in Table 1.

Endocrine-disrupting compounds (EDCs) is a term commonly used to describe these substances that potentially interfere with hormones. Until now, observations on the impact of EDCs mainly focused on vertebrates and steroid substances (Vos et al., 2000; OECD, 2001). Endocrine disruption has also been relatively well studied in aquatic invertebrates (OECD, 2005; LeBlanc et al., 1999; Depledge et al., 1994; Hutchinson, 2002) but hardly any information is available on soil invertebrates.

In this sense, the objective of this study was to investigate the sublethal effects of six IGRs on the springtail *Folsomia candida* (Willem) (Collembola; Isotomidae). Effects of methoprene, fenoxycarb, precocene II, tebufenozide, hexaflumuron, and teflubenzuron on the survival and reproduction rates of *F. candida* were evaluated. The impacts of fenoxycarb on the number of eggs laid and juveniles hatched were also evaluated. Furthermore, the effect of diuron, a herbicide of the urea chemical family, was tested on *F. candida* as this substance is known to potentially interfere with the androgen receptors of vertebrates (Bauer and Roembke, 1997; http://docs.pesticideinfo.org/Index.html, 2004).

The Materials and Methods section is presented in several sections, dealing in turn with information about the test organism and the breeding protocols, the chemicals used in the tests, the preparation and contamination of the substrate (artificial soil), survival and reproduction testing (experimental set-up), a compressed-soil experiment, and the statistical analyses.

2. Material and methods

2.1. Test organism

F. *candida* is an apterygote (wingless) arthropod belonging to the Collembola class which includes approximately 6500 species. It is a parthenogenic, unpigmented, and eyeless organism which can be found in most regions of the world except for Africa and India (Hopkin, 1997). Collembola have no metamorphosis and molt continuously throughout the entire life cycle. *F. candida* can reproduce after 12–16 days; the species has a high reproductive rate and can easily be bred in the laboratory (Spahr, 1981; Wiles and Krogh, 1998). Due to its importance to soil biology and to its key position in the soil food web (prey and consumer), *F. candida* is a relevant species for ecotoxicological testing (Laskowski et al., 1998; Fountain and Hopkin, 2001) and is the Collembola species used in the ISO standard 11267 (ISO, 1999). The Guidance document on terrestrial ecotoxicology (EC, 2002) and the Standards of the European and Mediterranean Plant Protection Organization (EPPO, 2003) recommend the use of this reproduction test with *F. candida* under certain circumstances as part of the EU pesticide assessment scheme.

2.2. Breeding of F. candida

The Collembola *F. candida* used for the experiments were generously provided by Dr. Frank Riepert from the Biologische Bundesanstalt für Land und Forstwirtschaft, Berlin, Germany and have been bred in our laboratory since 1996.
According to the ISO standard 11267 (ISO, 1999), *F. candida* were cultured in plastic containers (160× 110 × 60 mm with transparent cover). Recipients were

Notice in Section 2.5 that while there is much detail on how the substrates were prepared, the authors do not give details of standard lab protocols, such as how much stock solution was added to achieve the desired concentrations. Authors are expected to provide the level of detail necessary for someone to repeat the work (and also to assess the validity of the results and conclusions), while omitting unnecessary details and referring to the literature when possible. Section 2.6, on the experimental protocol, describes how the tests and controls were set up (only part of their text shown). Notice that they were following standards for using this organism in pesticide testing, as they explained in the section on the test organism.

2.5. Preparation and contamination of the substrate

Testing was conducted with artificial OECD soil (OECD, 1984). The soil was composed of 70% quartz sand (50% 40–100 mesh Fluka No. 84878 (Buchs, Switzerland) and 50% $\geqslant$230 mesh Fluka No. 83340), 20% kaolinite clay (Fluka No. 60609), and 10% sphagnum peat (Norddeutscher Hochmoortorf, pH 3.3; ESG-Bush GmbH, Rastede, Germany). The peat was air dried, ground, and sieved to 1 mm. Sufficient amount of $CaCO_3$ was added to reach a pH of 6 ± 0.5 (ISO, 1994). A quantity of bidistilled water corresponding to 50% of the water holding capacity (ISO, 1999) was added to the different soil constituents, which were mixed thoroughly.

For each experiment, the quantity of the stock solution required to obtain the desired concentrations was added to a volume of acetone equivalent to the total mass of quartz sand. The acetone was added to the quartz sand and mixed thoroughly. The mixture was rotary evaporated and then placed under a fume hood for 3 h to allow all acetone residues to evaporate. Finally, the contaminated quartz sand was mixed with the other soil constituents. All soils were prepared 1 day in advance and stored at room temperature.

2.6. Survival and reproduction testing

According to the ISO standard 11267 (ISO, 1999), substances were tested in a 28-day reproduction test. Preliminary range finder tests were conducted to determine the relevant test range of each substance. The concentrations finally tested are shown in Fig. 2. For each test, a control containing acetone was run in parallel. For fenoxycarb only, a test with compressed soil was conducted in addition to the ISO standard testing (see below).

Experiments according to the ISO standard were conducted in glass containers (diameter 4.5 cm, height 9.5 cm, with plastic covers closing tightly). Each container was filled with 30 g wet weight (ww) of artificial soil, without compressing the substrate. Ten juvenile springtails aged 10–12 days were introduced into each container. The containers were kept under the same conditions as the culture. They were opened twice per week to allow aeration. Approximately 10 mg of dry yeast was added at the beginning of the test (day 0) and 14 days later.

Five replicate containers were used for the control. Three replicates were used for each concentration (except for methoprene, hexaflumuron, and teflubenzuron where five replicates were used per concentration). Five additional test containers were prepared: four for

The Results section first documents the extent of compliance with the ISO standards (not reprinted here) and then summarizes the test findings, supporting the data with a table and two figures.

The 28-day data on the effects on reproduction (EC50 and EC10) and survival (LC50) and the corresponding no effect (NOEC) and lowest effect (LOEC) concentrations for each substance tested are shown in Table 2.

In the cases of methoprene and precocene II, effects on the mortality of the adults were observed at the same order of magnitude as the effect on the reproduction with an EC50 of 173 mg/kg soil (dry weight; dw) and a LC50 of 178 mg/kg for methoprene and an EC50 of 15 mg/kg and a LC50 of 26 mg/kg for precocene II.

	LC50	EC50	EC10	NOEC	LOEC
Methoprene	178.0 (168.2–194.7)	172.6 (159.5–185.5)	70.0 (33.6–147.2)	130.0	175.0
Fenoxycarb	>3052	113.2 (9.3–174.0)	2.4 (1.4–11.1)	12.5	31.5
Precocene II	25.7 (22.5–29.3)	14.8 (13.2–16.4)	3.7 (0.3–10.5)	8.8	12.8
Tebufenozide	>730	109.2 (n.c.)	9.2 (0–63.3)	9	20
Hexaflumuron	1.8 (1.5–2.6)	0.6 (0.4–0.7)	0.1 (0.03–0.23)	0.1	0.15
Teflubenzuron	0.22 (0.19–0.27)	0.05 (0.03–0.06)	0.004 (0–0.02)	0.007	0.02
Diuron	703.0 (451.1–1095.6)	19.7 (13.2–23.6)	0.7 (0.4–12.9)	10.0	25.0

n.c., not calculable.

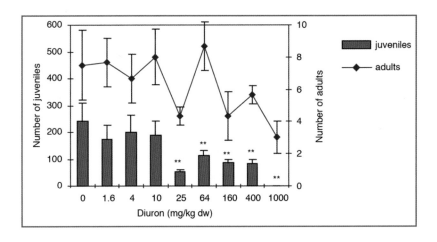

The Discussion begins by stating and evaluating the main finding.

4. Discussion

F. candida showed great differences in sensitivity to the different compounds tested. The chitin synthesis inhibitor teflubenzuron has the highest toxicity of all the tested substances for *F. candida* for both mortality and reproduction. No measured soil concentrations could be found in the literature for the tested compounds. To evaluate the obtained effect concentrations, an initial worst-case predicted environmental concentration (PEC_i) was estimated and compared to ecotoxicity values (Table 3). According to the EU directive on

Later in the discussion they address several comparisons between the treatments and between their results and the literature.

It is surprising that two juvenile hormone analogs such as fenoxycarb and methoprene show such large differences of toxicity for *F. candida*. These differences in toxicity might be due to two distinct molecular structures which do not have the same affinity for the receptor. The apparent similarity of methoprene to juvenile hormone is greater than the apparent similarity of fenoxycarb to juvenile hormone (Fig. 1). Methoprene is considered one of the most active juvenile hormone analogs for insects (Dhadialla et al., 1998). However, according to Edwards and Abraham (1985), fenoxycarb is 100 times more effective than methoprene for the Coleoptera *Alphitobius diaperinus*, which is not the case for *F. candida* with our results. Considering the wide variety of effects noted for these juvenile hormone-disrupting substances on insects (see Table 1), it is difficult to predict the exact mode of action in *F. candida*.

In this journal the format includes a separate section for conclusions. Here, the authors address their main hypothesis (that these pesticides impact Collembola) and additional findings (the variation in effects of different pesticides) and look to future work that needs to be done.

5. Conclusion

Although insect growth regulators were specifically developed to suppress pest insects, our results show that nontarget arthropods such as the Collembola *F. candida* are affected by these compounds. The two chitin synthesis inhibitors teflubenzuron and hexaflumuron were the most toxic compounds at concentrations that are probably environmentally relevant (toxicity/exposure ratios <5).

Juvenile hormone or ecdysone-disrupting substances have a wide variety of effects on insects (see Table 1). We have shown that compounds targeting the same hormone do not necessarily have the same effect. The wide range of effects and differences of sensitivity noted for these compounds seem to depend strongly on parameters such as receptor affinities, regulatory pathways, life stages, and taxa.

Our results do not enable elucidation of the exact mode of action of the tested compounds in *F. candida*. It is not clear whether the effect can be considered as endocrine disruption, which usually occurs at lower than sublethal concentrations. The elucidation of this question would need molecular approaches. However, effects of endocrine disruption may be ecologically irrelevant in the presence of other mechanisms of acute and/or chronic toxicity (Preston et al., 2000). The chronic effects observed in this study at environmentally relevant concentrations are of concern and could have consequences for the population of *F. candida* or other soil arthropods.

The paper ends with Acknowledgments and References.

References

Ayala, F.J. 2009. Darwin and the scientific method. *Proceedings of the National Academy of Sciences, USA* 106 (Suppl. 1): 10033–10039.

Campiche, S., Becker-van Slooten, K., Ridreau, C., & Tarradellas, J. 2006. Effects of insect growth regulators on the nontarget soil arthropod *Folsomia candida* (Collembola). *Ecotoxicology and Environmental Safety* 63: 216–225.

Darwin, F. 1903. *More Letters of Charles Darwin*. Murray, London.

Gastel, B. & Day, R.A. 2016. *How to Write and Publish a Scientific Paper*, 8th ed. Greenwood Press, Westport, CT.

Gopen, G. & Swan, J. 1990. The science of scientific writing. *American Scientist* 78: 550–558. [Official version online at www.americanscientist .org/issues/feature/the-science-of-scientific-writing/1], accessed 20 June 2016.

Halliday, M.A.K. & Martin, J. R. 1993. *Writing Science: Literacy and Discursive Power*. University of Pittsburgh Press, Pittsburgh, PA.

Hannam, S. & Rutowski, R. n.d. The peppered moth: A seasoned survivor. https://askabiologist.asu.edu/why-vs-how-biology, accessed 1 June 2016.

Hyland, K. 1998. *Hedging in Scientific Research Articles*. John Benjamins Publishing, Amsterdam.

Hyland, K. 2004. *Disciplinary Discourses: Social Interactions in Academic Writing*. University of Michigan Press, Ann Arbor, MI.

Lemke, J.L. 1990. *Talking Science: Language, Learning, and Values*. Ablex Publishing, Norwood, NJ.

Lobban, C.S., Schefter, M., Camacho, F.A., & Jocson, J. 2014. *Tropical Pacific Island Environments*, 2nd ed. Bess Press, Honolulu, HI.

Love, A. 1996. How do we explain explanation? An examination of the concept of "explanation" in relation to the communication needs of science undergraduates. In Hewings, M. & Dudley-Evans, T. (eds.), *Evaluation and Course Design in EAP*. Prentice Hall-Macmillan in association with the British Council, Hemel Hempstead, pp. 151–165.

Mayr, E. 1982. *The Growth of Biological Thought: Diversity, Evolution, and Inheritance*. Belknap Press of Harvard University Press, Cambridge, MA.

Palacios-Vargas, J.G., Castaño-Meneses, G., Gómez-Anaya, J.A., Martínez-Yrizar, A., Mejía-Recamia, B.E., & Martínez-Sanchez, J. 2007. Litter and soil arthropods diversity and density in a tropical dry forest ecosystem in Western Mexico. *Biodiversity and Conservation* 16: 3703–3717.

Paul, R. & Elder, L. n.d. Elements and standards learning tool. www.critical thinking.org/pages/elements-and-standards-learning-tool/783, accessed 23 December 2012.

Roig, M. 2015. Avoiding plagiarism, self-plagiarism, and other questionable writing practices: A guide to ethical writing. US Department of Health and Human Services, Office of Research Integrity. http://ori.hhs.gov/sites/default/files/plagiarism.pdf, accessed 21 September 2016.

Romero, L.M. & Wikelski, M. 2010. Stress physiology as a predictor of survival in Galàpagos marine iguanas. *Proceedings of the Royal Society B* 277: 3157–3162.

Schefter, M. 1996. Student reactions to tentative language (hedging) in genres of environmental science writing. PhD Dissertation, The Union Institute, Cincinnati, OH.

Swales, J.M. 1990. *Genre Analysis: English in Academic and Research Settings.* Cambridge University Press, Cambridge.

Swales, J.M. 2004. *Research Genres: Explorations and Applications.* Cambridge University Press, Cambridge.

Thierry, B. 2005. Integrating proximate and ultimate causation: Just one more go! *Current Science* 89: 1180–1183.

Woodford, F.P. (ed.) 1968. *Scientific Writing for Graduate Students.* Council of Biology Editors, Bethesda, MD.

Further Reading

Cargill, M. & O'Connor, P. 2013. *Writing Scientific Research Articles: Strategy and Steps*, 2nd ed. Wiley-Blackwell, Chichester.

Council of Science Editors. 2014. *Scientific Style and Format: The CSE Manual for Authors, Editors, and Publishers*, 8th ed. Council of Science Editors, Wheat Ridge, CO.

Glasman-Deal, H. 2010. *Science Research Writing for Non-native Speakers of English*. Imperial College Press, London.

Greene, A.E. 2013. *Writing Science in Plain English (Chicago Guides to Writing, Editing, and Publishing)*. University of Chicago Press, Chicago, IL.

Hoffman, A. 2014. *Scientific Writing and Communication: Papers, Proposals, and Presentations*, 2nd ed. Oxford University Press, Oxford.

Lindsay, D. 2011. *Scientific Writing = Thinking in Words*. CSIRO Publishing, Collingwood, VIC.

Matthews, J.R. & Matthews, R.W. 2015. *Successful Scientific Writing: A Step-by-Step Guide for the Biological and Medical Sciences*, 4th ed. Cambridge University Press, Cambridge.

McMillan, V.E. 2012. *Writing Papers in the Biological Sciences*, 5th ed. Bedford/St. Martin's Press, Boston, MA.

Schimel, J. 2011. *Writing Science: How to Write Papers that Get Cited and Proposals that Get Funded*. Oxford University Press, Oxford.

Turabian, K.L. & Booth, W.C. 2013. *A Manual for Writers of Term Papers, Theses, and Dissertations*, 8th ed. University of Chicago Press, Chicago, IL.

Index